Julius Woldemar Zeibig, Norman Peter Heffley

Ancient and Medieval Shorthand

Julius Woldemar Zeibig, Norman Peter Heffley

Ancient and Medieval Shorthand

ISBN/EAN: 9783744744256

Printed in Europe, USA, Canada, Australia, Japan

Cover: Foto ©ninafisch / pixelio.de

More available books at **www.hansebooks.com**

MEDIÆVAL SHORTHAND;

— FROM —

DR. J. W. ZEIBIG'S

Geschichte der Geschwindschreibkunst,

— BY —

N. P. HEFFLEY,

MEMBER OF THE INTERNATIONAL SHORTHAND CONGRESS, AND THE STOLZE STENO-
GRAPHIC SOCIETY OF BERLIN, GERMANY; ASSOCIATE MEMBER OF THE SHORTHAND
SOCIETY. LONDON ; HONORARY MEMBER OF THE N. Y. STATE STENOGRAPHERS'
ASSOCIATION AND OF THE NEBRASKA STENOGRAPHERS' ASSOCIATION.

(Re-printed from the Proceedings of the N. Y. State Stenographers' Ass'n for 1887.)

BROOKLYN, N. Y.
1888.

PREFACE.

$\mathcal{H}$AVING been greatly interested in the historical aspects of short-hand ever since beginning its study, I undertook, some years ago, to compile a detailed and impartial history of "Stenography and Phonography, or Shorthand." Since the publication by me of the "Biography of the Father of Stenography," etc., for the purpose of ascertaining whether the interest in the history of this art would justify the publication of the detailed work, as outlined, various causes have prevented its entire completion. Moreover, the little interest generally manifested concerning the *history* of the art has rather discouraged the preparation and publication of the proposed work.

Solely as an aid in my investigations, I translated, in 1882, that portion of Dr. Zeibig's celebrated work* which relates to ancient shorthand ; this work being the most complete, in this respect, of any history of the art published in any modern language. In view of the proposed celebration of the Jubilee of Phonography and Tercentenary of Shorthand at London next September, and in the hope of creating an increased interest in the history of the art, I have concluded to publish this translation, adding, in foot notes, renditions of the more important Latin passages occurring in the original. If this hope shall be realized, I shall at some future time issue a fuller and more exhaustive work upon the history of shorthand from the most ancient to the present time.

Brooklyn, N. Y., August 1, 1887.   N. P. H.

---

* Geschichte und Literatur der Geschwindschreibkunst von Dr. Julius Woldemar Zeibig, Professor am Königl. stenografischen Institut zu Dresden. Herausgegeben vom Königl. stenografischen Institut zu Dresden. Zweite, vermehrte, verbesserte und mit 41 Tafeln versehene Auflage. Dresden. Verlag von Gustav Dietze. 1878.

INTRODUCTION.

It needs no authority for the statement that writing had to climb many steps of simplification before it reached its climax—tachygraphy. The older a nation, and the more elaborate and unhandy its writing, the more difficult and perplexing became the path which led to this object. Among nations of antiquity, the Romans alone, and in their later days, the Greeks, seem to have developed a quick-writing. But with regard to their systems, we may well exclaim with Tacitus: "Everything was not better with our forefathers; "our age also has produced much that is praiseworthy and of use " for coming generations."

Interesting as it is to trace the art of writing from its first inception to the invention which reduced it to its greatest simplicity, we must only consider so much of the history of its development as appears indispensably necessary to a better understanding of the several methods. As regards the various appellations and definitions of tachygraphy, the majority of these will be discussed in their respective places. We may refrain from referring to them in advance for the further reason, that, in spite of the manifold terminology, the aim which the inventor of every system of tachygraphy has in view is one and the same, namely : to offer to every one the possibility to write as quickly as one speaks, and with such accuracy that at any time the writing can, not only be read by himself as common writing, but also that others conversant with the system may be able to read it.

To show what exertions have from time to time been made, and by whom, in order to attain this end, is the object of this history of stenography.

THE ALLEGED AGE OF THE ART OF SHORTHAND WRITING.

Καὶ ἐς μὲν ἀκρόασιν ἴσως τὸ μὴ μυθῶδες
αὐτῶν ἀτερπέστερον φανεῖται.

—Thucydides.

THE first inquiry as to how far the invention and practice of shorthand writing dates back into antiquity, has been answered with suppositions and assertions which cannot be maintained when more carefully investigated.

People are very apt to trace the origin of an art into the obscurity of the earliest times, in order to make it more venerable. Gabelsberger, in the first edition of his Guide, traces the art of shorthand writing to the earliest times of writing practice. In the very beginning of the use of writing, he finds the highest development. In the second edition of this Guide, made up from his posthumous papers, scarcely anything is found of the historical material of the first edition, a fact which perhaps justifies the presumption that the author himself may have entertained doubts as to the correctness of the statements made in his earlier work. Nevertheless, the subsequent editors of his system did not entertain such doubts respecting the history of stenography, and almost all of them have repeated the essential statements that were contained in the first edition. If, therefore, my investigation of the question : Does the art of shorthand writing date back as far into antiquity as has been alleged? is attended with different results than appear in the writings of my predecessors in this field of historical research, no one, I hope, will accuse me of irreverence to Gabelsberger, or condemn the hand which destroys the halo discovered to be false. If, however, contrary to my belief, some one should accuse me, I will say to him : " Truth is more to me than Plato and Aristotle."

That the ancient Egyptians did not know the art of shorthand writing (which people were inclined to believe in former times) can easily be established by making ourselves acquainted with the systems of writing used by that people. This erroneous hypothesis has, therefore, rightfully been rejected by Dr. Anders.

When Gesenius infers from the change in the form of the written signs of the Phœnicians the existence of shorthand writing among that people, he can only have had the current writing in mind. The Phœnicians had but a poor literature. We have knowledge only of a few monumental inscriptions or priest's books. Their merchants, who were the disseminators of writing along the Mediterranean, wrote to suit their own purposes and naturally made use of briefer signs than those found on the monuments of stone and metal. The necessity for a real shorthand writing did not exist then, and nothing justifies the assumption that it did. But the evidence which Gesenius adduces for his opinion of the alleged existence of tachygraphers among the Hebrews, is, as we shall presently show, entirely insupportable.

Further, we read : " Xerxes, for a quicker execution of his com " mands, employed shorthand writers." In Herodotus, upon whom they seem to base this statement, we search in vain for a confirmation thereof. The only passages which possibly might have led to such a view are the following: In the 7th book we read : " After Xerxes " had his army counted and mustered he wished to inspect it him " self; he seated himself in a chariot and visited all the various na

"tionalities of which the army was composed. Each of these
" nationalities he investigated, and made inquiries about their circum-
"stances, *and his writers noted down the information he received*, until
" he had passed from one end to the other and had seen all his in-
"fantry and cavalry. Then he ordered the ships to go to sea, and,
"alighting from his chariot, entered into a Sidonian vessel and
" seated himself under a gold woven tent. He passed in front of
" every vessel and put the same questions which he had addressed
" to the army, to the various divisions of the fleet, and had the an-
"swers, likewise, written down." In the 3rd book it is said that
" the subordinate generals all had royally appointed writers." Both
of these passages can only be *forcibly* strained into proof that shorthand writers existed among the ancient Persians. Does this need
any further comment?

The supposition that the Hebrews knew and practiced the art of
shorthand writing has no better foundation. As a proof that
" among these people, the foundation and elaboration of the higher
" art of shorthand writing, based upon abbreviations of writing, is
" mainly to be sought," Gabelsberger adduces as his authorities Bib-
liander and Rader. Although the words of the former, under the
heading, *de notis*, and those of the latter, in a translation of the well-
known epigram of Martial upon a quick writer, merely suggest that
abbreviations were used, while from the tenor of these authors'
works they seem to have considered these abbreviations as shorthand writing, nothing follows from this but the fact that the
Hebrews used letters for syllables and words, and words for whole
sentences; a mode of abbreviation which was also in use among
other nations, but is by no means necessarily connected with a sys-
tematic art. Moreover, how do we know that the Hebrews used the
above named abbreviations for stenographic purposes, and not rather,
as appears far more probable, for the purpose of secret writing?
Equally weak are the supports given and based upon the passages
quoted from the Bible and the apocryphal 4th book of Ezra. Neither
the xlvth Psalm, verse 1 : " My tongue *is* the pen of a ready writer ;"
nor Jeremiah, Chap. xxxvi, verses 4 and 18 : " Then Jeremiah called
" Baruch the son of Neriah: and Baruch wrote from the mouth of
" Jeremiah all the words of the Lord, which he had spoken unto
" him, upon a roll of a book,"—"He pronounced all these words
" unto me with his mouth, and I wrote them with ink in the book,"—
impel us to think of shorthand writers.

The Hebrew word מָהִיר in that passage of the Psalm may
mean " conversant " as well as " quick," but " write from the
mouth " is nothing else than writing from dictation ; and as regards
the proof of the passages from the so-called 4th book of Ezra,
which read as follows : " But thou take with thee many tablets and
take with thee Sareas, Dabrias, Semelias, Echanas and Asiel, these

five men, because they are ready to write," ("skilled in quick writing"); but in the 40 days 94 (204) books were written," we have to oppose the fact that this alleged book of Ezra, which was compiled from 94 to 95 A. D. by a Jew who knew how to imitate skilfully the older prophets, only exists in translations—a Latin, an Arabic and an Ethiopian-Abyssinian; that the texts of these translations in many instances differ from one another, not even all of them containing the book complete; that the translation which is referred to by the opposing demonstrators is the most corrupted; and that, finally, even apart from all this, no plausible reason exists which compels us to recognize in the above named five writers, shorthand writers, but merely writers of common writing, who generally or always were found among the Hebrews, carrying their writing materials with them in a belt fastened to a little chain. The argument which Gabelsberger borrows from the quantity of matter the five writers wrote in 40 days is considerably shaken when we read instead of the Latin translation, which is "*ducenti quatuor*," 204, the other and better texts, "*nonaginta quatuor*," 94, for in that case not quite one-half of a book, instead of more than a whole book, comes to the share of each writer. But since a "book" is a most indefinite quantity with regard to volume and contents, and according to the mode of expression of those days corresponds to our "paragraph" or "chapter," evidence based upon such vague expressions is of course no proof. Nowhere do we find distinct mention of shorthand writers in any of the writings of the Jews before the birth of Christ, while such allusion naturally should be expected if the art had flourished among that people in those days. Neither do we meet any express references to the art among Jewish authors of a later period. The Hebrews preserved with a faithful conscientiousness everything pertaining to their theocracy up to the destruction of Jerusalem. This adherence to earlier things went to the extent of petty pedantry. Had they once had a stenographic alphabet they would have preserved it. The suppositious statement at one time attributed to St. Paul "that even at the courts of the temple and synagogue of "Jerusalem, a kind of shorthand writers were employed as record-"ers, and that, from documents of this kind, the Christians might "have collected copies after the death of Jesus; especially, as schol-"ars and priests were found among the adherents of Jesus,"—lacks all historical foundation, as Wegscheider, in our opinion, has fully demonstrated.

Finally, Gabelsberger acknowledges and regrets, as does also Anders, that positive proofs of real Hebrew shorthand writing have not been handed down to our times. But as the evidence furnished in support of the views contested by us, has not proven tenable, we have no reason to wonder at the fact that hitherto no evidence of Hebrew tachygraphy has been found. This fact rather tends to sustain our doubts as to the existence of this art in Judea.

As to the alleged possession of shorthand writing by the ancient Indians, enough has been said by Dr. Mitzschke. He has demonstrated that there cannot consistently be any talk of an Indian stenography. The same author refutes the opinion that the existence of shorthand writing among the Armenians can be inferred from the words of the Armenian evangelist, Agathangelos, (who died 352): " The secretaries of the king Tiridates noted down with signs every- "thing that the holy man spoke," and again, "they came thither, " and after they had noted down with signs all the words of the " saints, they read the same to the king."

The Chinese possess among their three forms of writing a sort of quick writing called tsaò schû, or grass writing, in which the writing pencil does not leave the paper, and in which the various individual strokes, of which a character consists, are made in one movement. The brush which describes the direction of the several strokes gives also an outline of a character, but without any very distinct expression of details. The tsaò writing is tachygraphy, and space is not spared. The written strokes appear in manifold twistings, so that it requires not a little practice and a considerable knowledge of the language to be able to read these signs, allowing much scope to the will of the writer to bring forth many very peculiar characters with each stroke of the brush. · This mode of writing is said to date from the period of the Han dynasty. Its invention is ascribed to the various scholars who lived during the period from 48 to 80 A. D. As regards Japan, writing there was at first with Chinese characters, but subsequently these were abbreviated, and only individual characteristic elements were taken and used as phonetic signs. From the printed characters arose the Katakana, and from the quick writing the Hiragana. Stenographic, that is, space-saving signs, often occurred in epistolary style for frequently occurring words. In our days, a manual of tachygraphy is said to have been published at Yokohama, but inquiries made directly at the Japanese embassy at Berlin cause us to doubt the existence in Japan of a stenography in its more restricted sense.

The modern Persians likewise possess a sort of quick writing. Wilken in his " Rudiments of the Persian Language," (Leipsig, 1805) says in regard to it : " In their letters they frequently omit, " especially in intelligently written compositions, diacritical points " of sentences ; this they call Schekestheh, that is, broken sentence " writing." Furthermore, we read, with regard to the nature and the use of this writing, in the " Phonetic Journal " (1869, P. 146): " Is is used in all the courts of law, and it is found quite sufficient " for the purpose of taking down the evidence of witnesses. As " making set speeches is a thing almost unknown in India, there has " never been a necessity felt for anything more rapid than this " shikest. I have often been present when the magistrate's clerk

" (Sheristatar) was taking down the actual spoken evidence of some
" native witness, and I have found it, afterwards, to be quite ver-
" batim.   They leave out all the vowels, just as we do.   I cannot say
" much for the legibility of their reports.   I am sure of one thing ;
" they would never be fit to go to press ; but in the matter of speed,
" this system of writing is but little behind our own.   To obtain a
" degree in this branch of learning is looked upon as a great honor,
" and this degree, which is called Chisnovisi, is considered quite as
" grand a thing to attain as our degree of LL. D."

In an article headed " On the Tachygraphy of the Greeks," in the
periodical " Hermes" 11th volume, pages 443 to 457, Dr. Gardthausen, of Leipzig, endeavors to refute the supposition that the introduction of stenography among the Greeks was antedated by stenography among the Romans.   He expresses himself thus :   " Still
" more perplexing than the variety of opinions regarding the time of
" the invention of the Grecian tachygraphy, is the supposition that
" the Tironean Notes were the very prototype of Grecian tachygra-
" phy, for not only would thereby the relation of giving and taking,
" as in fact it existed between the two nations, be completely (?) re-
" versed, but that we find the Greek letters in the Tironean alphabet
" would also be inexplicable."   Mr. Gardthausen can not dispute
the possibility that the rules of giving and taking in a special case
could have been reversed without thereby *completely* reversing the relation of giving and taking.   But the appearance of Greek letters in
the Tironean alphabet, is not strange to him who remembers that
the lists of Tironean Notes did not originate at the same time with
the alphabet.   The subsequent introduction of Greek words into the
note commentaries was the occasion for the employment of Greek
letters.   Has it, in fact, been otherwise with the common Latin
alphabet, which orignally contained neither the aspirates nor the
letters z or y ?   Again, Mr. Gardthausen says :   " But what surprises
" us most is that the practical requirements of the Greeks should not
" have led to this invention; inasmuch as wherever judicial and po-
" litical eloquence exists, this invention naturally suggests itself."
Mr. Gardthausen does not mention that others before him had entertained the same view, nor that on page 9 of the history of the art of
quick-writing, discussions are found referring to actual counter reasons,
for which a Greek tachygraphy could not be claimed at so early a period
as Mr. Gardthausen thinks.   In this case, all should have been spe-
cially refuted that has been adduced in other places, according to
Schneider's precedent, against the supposition that ὑποσημειοῦσθαι
means stenography.   Mr. Gardthausen, while occupying himself exclusively with the passage of Diogenes of Laertius, referring to
Xenophon, wholly ignores the parallel expression, ὑποσημειώσεις
ἐποιεῖτο, explanatory of : ὑποσημειοῦσθαι, which the same Diogenes
uses with reference to the mnemotechnic (ὧν ἐμνημόνευεν) minutes,

which the Athenian σχυτοτόμος Simon made of the colloquies of Socrates ! Hence, it is obvious that in the passage of Diogenes the ὑποσημειοῦσθαι, in consequence of the well-known significations of the preposition ὑπὸ, may mean either to make " jottings, or noting-down, without the knowledge of others ;" or, as seems more likely, " before and after writing." So long as it has not been proven, and Mr. Gardthausen has forgotten to prove it, that this conception and translation of the passages of Diogenes are false, it remains simply an uncorroborated assertion that ὑποσημειῶ is a technical expression for tachygraphically noting down. It is difficult to see, without *petitio principii*, how, in the words from the Church history of Eusebius, page 283A, and from the letters of Pliny, 1, 10, an allusion to tachygraphic notes can be found. Obviously, the preposition ὑπὸ in this case, just as the Latin *sub* in *subnoto* (and *subsigno*) in Pliny, retains its original literary signification, so that ὑποσημειοῦσθαι in Eusebius and *subnoto* (*subsigno*) in Pliny are synonymous with ὑπογράφεω and *subscribere*, a relationship which is apparent in other passages as well, and also between the nouns ὑποσημείωσις and ὑπογραφή, *subsignatio* and *subscriptio* respectively, the same as in our " undersigned " and " underwritten." So when, further, Mr. Gardthausen, in proof of his assertion, refers to the fact that a number of papygraphical documents have become known which contain tachygraphic notes ; and in this respect especially points out the explanation of an Egyptian document on papyrus, published in the year 1821 by Böckh, in which explanation we read : " Among others, an illegible signature not written with the common " letters, but with tachygraphic notes, like the Tironean Notes " of the Romans. Of this speciés Kopp, Tach. vett. I, 435, &c., " says: I did not succeed, however, in deciphering this signature by " comparing it with the notes edited by him. I might have been inclined to suppose that the name Apollonios is contained in the " features of the latter kind of writing ;" but when he, contrary to Böckh and Leemans, explains this signature as a tachygraphical designation of the names Κλεοπάτρα Πτολεμαῖος, and in so doing believes himself to have proven the great age of Grecian tachygraphy, then we have ground to strongly doubt the correctness of this deciphering.

If, indeed, all these individual letters are expressed in the written characters of the Böckh papyrus, then, it is at best a tachygraphy no more deserving the name than our so-called small Greek and Latin letters would deserve that name when used as abbreviations of the corresponding majusculæ (capital letters). But this is at least not tachygraphy or stenography of the kind found in the Tironean Notes. The nature of stenography consists in the simplification and at the same time the omission of letters. While, therefore, the ancient Latin stenography writes C (o) P (t) a, for Cleopatra and P (o) L M us, for Ptolemus, thus only designating the main consonants together with the respective terminations ; the Greek tachygraphy, the alleged prototype of the Roman, is claimed to have brought out expression of all individual letters. If advanced to such completeness of phonetic writing, Greek tachygraphy would have gone far beyond, not only ancient, but the later invented Latin syllable stenography. Now regarding the alleged undersigned names themselves! That the Böckh papyrus originates from the year 105 B. C. (not 104—see Böckh's Monograph V, 208 and 214), is certainly without doubt. On the other hand, it requires an unusual degree of credulity to suppose that the names of officers or other interested parties are not there (compared with the signatures of the third section : $\Delta\iota\ [o\nu\acute{o}\sigma\iota\varsigma]\ \tau\rho\alpha\pi\varepsilon\xi\acute{\iota}\tau\eta\varsigma$), but, that the names of two royal personages should be found as signatures to these documents concerning the sale of a lot of ground which passed from the hands of Pamonthes, Enachomneus, Sam. Persinei, M. Persinci, into the hands of the Nechutes! And why should the signatures of the two royal personages be signed at the end of a document concerning a sale in which these persons, according to the contents of the document, were not in any way interested? If "the royal street" appears as the southern limit of the estate (if the word "$\dot{\rho}\acute{o}\mu\eta$" is properly read) that does not prove any title to or participation in the deed by the persons named, while the rather voluminous text which forms the beginning of the document appears a chronological abstract, or some similar signification, such as the first words of our notarial instruments. The better supposition is, that in the signature, the "demotic" manner of writing occurs, for the deciphering of which the Egyptologists may render useful service. In short, the proof for the antedate of Greek tachygraphy in opposition to the Latin, has not been produced ; and whether Greek priority can be shown by the papyrii in Paris, Leyden and Berlin, remains to be seen.

WHO WAS THE INVENTOR ?

"Who, then, was the inventor of sign-writing?" asks Lipsius in his well-known letter to Lessius, and he answers this question with the words : " I would award the fame to the Greeks and especially to "the philosopher and historian Xenophon, of whom Diogenes says : "' He was the first *to note* down the sayings of Socrates and to "publish them.'" This passage in Diogenes Laertius seems to have given an impulse to the view hitherto deemed incontrovertible, that Xenophon had tachygraphed the speeches of Socrates. Why should we then wonder that this art flourished among the ancient Greeks? "The ardent wish to have the lectures of such famous "teachers, the orations of such distinguished men, in the public "assemblies, verbatim, was a natural one. These lectures could be

"heard only by a small portion of the people; but it was desirable
"to bring them speedily to the knowledge of the whole people, and
"many a one who himself had heard these most beautiful produc-
"tions of spontaneous inspiration and enthusiasm, felt a necessity to
"fix them and preserve them for subsequent generations. This re-
"quirement was fully met by stenography." Does it not seem quite
self-evident that this important art was considered an independent
branch and was taught in the schools? Is it not more than probable
that beside the orations of the philosophers and the statesmen, the
court proceedings and those of the council of the "Amphictyons"
were also noted down by shorthand writers? Was not the "golden
age of Greece" also the prime period of Greek shorthand writing?

Natural and well-founded as this whole train of ideas may appear,
we doubt the correctness of these hitherto prevalent views concerning
the antiquity of the art, and cannot refrain from stating our contradictory conviction, and are ready to present our proof.

As has been intimated before, this whole fabric of ingenius hypotheses and inferences is based upon a passage in Diogenes Laertius,
an author who lived about the middle of the third century of our
era. The above given versions of this author have been translated
very differently into Latin. That translation in which a tachygraphic *noting down* of the sayings of Socrates *is not* claimed, is indis-
putably the correct one, for in the meaning of the words ὑποσημείωω
or ὑποσημειόομαι there is not the slightest allusion to any *quick*
writing; it only means to "note down," not to write down *tachygraphically.* Even in other languages, cultivated as well as barbar-
ous, "to make signs" is equivalent to "writing." That we cannot
be justified in inferring the existence of a tachygraphy with the ancient Greeks upon the ground of the frequently mentioned passages
of Diogenes, or even by the alleged fact that Xenophon was the inventor of the same, has already been expressed by Schneider in his
edition of the "Xenophonic Notables." He says: "He who first
"translated ἀπομνημονεύματα as '*memorabilia*,' whether it was by
"Victorius, or whoever else, has neither expressed himself in good
"Latin nor faithfully rendered the meaning of the word. The word
"itself proves that the observation of Weiske is erroneous, when he,
"(because Diogenes Laertius says that Xenophon had noted down
"what he narrates about Socrates) refers to this quotation as a proof
"of tachygraphy, and tells us that through its practice Xenophon
"had been enabled to note down and publish the speeches of
"Socrates, and, like Lipsius, (letter 27 of the 1st hundred to the Bel-
"gians) makes Xenophon the inventor of tachygraphy. The
"learned gentleman should have remembered what he himself says
"subsequently, quoting from Diogenes, of Simon, a pupil of Soc-
"rates, who, as soon as he had left his teacher, *noted down* every-
"thing that he could *remember.* The opinions of those who claim

2

" that the art of quick writing was invented in the age of Xenophon,
" and even go so far as to make this philosopher the inventor of
" ' shorthand,' are simply absurd." Golden words, which like the
voice of the preacher in the wilderness, have died away unnoticed !
The second passage in Diogenes to which Schneider refers, is found
in Chap. xiii, book 2nd, and reads as follows : " Simon, of
" Athens, the shoemaker, wrote down as often as Socrates came to
" his workshop and had conversation with him, *all that he remem-*
" *bered.*" Thus the cobbler Simon *wrote down from his memory* the
speeches or talks which Socrates had had with him. In both passages, of Xenophon as of Simon, Diogenes uses the word
ὑποσημειόομαι. But we see plainly and clearly that neither here
nor there, tachygraphic writing is to be thought of, and that neither the
ἀπομνημονεύματα, (memorabilia) of Xenophon, nor the σχυτιχοὶ
διαλόγοι, (the cobbler's conversations) are based upon any *shorthand*
writing !

No more are we justified in thinking that those were stenographers,
who, at the command of Phillip of Macedon, noted down the humor-
ous speeches which the Club of Sixty made at Diomea, a suburb of
Athens, at the carnival of Hercules.

Among stenographers, Lewis seems to have been the first who
doubted the correctness of the time hallowed opinion contested by
us. Isaac Pitman also says in his History of Shorthand: " Diogenes
" Laertius has been made to say that Xenophon first took down the
" sayings of Socrates in notes, but the original text may mean that
" he merely noted down the sayings of Socrates." After we thus
have sufficiently shown that the evidence of quick writing as supposed to have flourished among the ancient Greeks, cannot consistently be based upon the frequently mentioned passage of Diogenes,
we next ask whether anywhere else in the writings of that people evidence exists in support of that assumption?

" Apart from the great historians and orators of the Greek people,
" who must ever be regarded as the foundation and source of erudition,
" there appears to be a lack of allusions to public life in some of the
" writings of the remaining authors of that period, and when this
" spirit faded away it was replaced by learned efforts to collect ma-
" terial, the result of which we now find partly embodied in the com-
" mentaries on authors of the classical period and partly in the works
" of the lexicographers Pollux, Harpocrates, Hesychius, Suidas, &c."
These compilations of the public as well as the private lives of the
Greeks furnish us with material for exhaustive information. The
most insignificant matters not worthy of mention were taken up and
preserved ; such, for instance, as the skill of Kallikratides and Myrme-
kides, who wrote a plaintive distich with golden letters upon a grain
of sesame, &c. !

If we consider what value and significance the art of oratory had in Greece;—that it was the constant companion of statesmanship; if we consider (which is undoubtedly the case) that mention was made in the writings of the ancients and by the commentators on the same, of all particulars regarding public oratory,—then it is equally sure that so powerful an innovation as shorthand writing, the best servant of oratory, *would have been mentioned, not merely incidentally, but specifically,* if this art had really been invented and practiced in Greece before the days of Cicero. If we succeed in furnishing the evidence of such omission, which, in this connection, is especially important, then we have virtually refuted the testimony of our opponents and proven their argumentative premises untenable.

Primarily, let us ask:. If a contemporary of Xenophon knew anything about tachygraphy, how is it that no one alluded to this art ? We even find a passage from which proof *against* the existence of this art can easily be adduced. We allude to the words of Thucydides: "As "regards the speeches made by the individuals, either when they "were about to begin the war or when they were fairly in it, it was "difficult for me to retain in the memory with accuracy that which "had been spoken and heard by myself, as well as that which was "reported to me from other places; but as the individuals, according "to my opinion, seem to have spoken most appropriately upon the "subject in question, I shall here give, as nearly as possible, the "whole meaning or sense of what was said."

If the art of shorthand writing had been current in Greece, we are justly astonished that Thucydides, one of the best informed and most distinguished men of Athens, was ignorant of this art or did not avail himself of it, when its particular use was that of recording speeches verbatim! Instead, we hear him complain of difficulties in reproducing the speeches he had heard, *from memory.* But it was not only himself who felt the want of shorthand ; all his reporters and friends as well (and he had such in various parts of Greece) could not report to him the accurate wording of the speeches. He expressly declares that it was impossible for him to render the orations with sharp accuracy—and yet it is claimed that the art of shorthand writing was known to the Greeks at that time!

As in the case of Thucydides, all subsequent Greek historians reproduced the speeches of their heroes from memory; nowhere amongst them do we find an authentic oration.

We find the same record in regard to the Grecian political orators themselves. As far as our information of their orations goes, from the prime of oratory to its decline, nowhere is allusion made to the art of quick-writing. On the other hand, among the Romans after Cicero's time, stenographers are mentioned, praised and censured.

Though the silence of the Greek authors concerning stenography proves sufficiently the non-existence of this art at that time, we have to draw further proofs for the truth of our assertion from the nature of the oratory of the ancients. Let us for that purpose examine the fate of the speeches, if we may use the phrase, from their inception to their publication! We know that whoever could avoid it, did not extemporize. Of the powerful orator Demosthenes, Plutarch relates that he often was urged to speak by the multitude, but that he never uttered a word unless he had thoroughly prepared himself. All speeches, before being delivered, were prepared with the greatest care. Then they were delivered at a favorable moment with the employment of all the aids of the so-called physical oratory, which even the greatest of orators did not disdain to make use of, the aquirement and proper use of which formed a special study. The effect of these speeches, naturally, greatly depended on the momentary moods of the multitude, and on the wise use of the same, as well as on declamation and gesticulation. Even tachygraphy, if it had been invented and practiced in those days, would not have been able to catch the volatile spirit and charm of the oration, which constituted, perhaps, one-half of its force. Those orators spoke for their hearers, not for readers. For the latter, these same speeches, if well received, were once more carefully elaborated and preserved, as monuments of oratorical art. Dionysius of Halikarnassus, makes no difference between the edited and copied orations ; his full remarks on the speeches and their style presuppose throughout their written composition, while after the invention of tachygraphy, the application of the same for the verbatim noting down of speeches, is often mentioned. Thus Plutarch (who, in the life of the younger Cato, expresses thanks to the instrumentality of Cicero that a speech of Cato had been noted down by quick writers and in this way was preserved), knows nothing of any such writing down of any speech of Demosthenes.

As regards the administration of justice among the Greeks, tachygraphy was not in use up to Cicero's time.

It is doubtful and even improbable that speeches were made at the sessions of the Diœtetes courts. At the sessions of the *Areopagus* the plaintiffs and defendants were allowed to make two speeches each, but they had to be delivered extempore, and had to be free from all irrelevant matter and oratorical ornamentation. "Make no long prologue and abstain from all ornamentation," cried the herald to the speakers. In neither of these cases was there a necessity to preserve the details of these short proceedings. The real theatre of judicial oratory was no doubt in the *Helliastic* tribunals. Here each party was entitled to take the floor twice. The time allowed for each speech was measured by a water-clock. Those who had no talents for composing such a speech had one written for money by a *logographer*, or they applied for that purpose to a friend. The tendency of the speech aimed especially at exciting the emotions and fanning the passions, sometimes that of scorn, sometimes that of pity. In these tribunals, if anywhere, the art of shorthand writing would have been employed if this important auxiliary of eloquence had been known at the time. The civil service in Greece was as varied and systematically organized as in any modern State. Pollux composed a list of the public writers in Athens. "In the various branches of public "administration," says Wachsmuth, "where writing was a neces-"sity, there were numerous employees, as is to be expected "of a people who were so fertile in literary productions of "all kinds, and among whom the humblest knew how to write. "Consequently, there must have been considerable difference in "rank from the chief writers of the State down to the writer for a "livelihood."

But nowhere is mention made of tachygraphers who noted down court proceedings at the command of the judges, or served as short-hand recorders, or even as note takers in the interest of the public in *causes célèbres*, which, as we know, were of quite frequent occurrence, whilst, after the birth of Christ, mention is repeatedly made of competent quick writers, who were on duty in the courts of justice. We refer here, among others, to the words of Proäresius in Eunapius: "I wish that quick writers be given to me and assigned to a "place before the eyes of all, that they may daily note down the sen-"tences of Themis; while, this day, I want them to follow me word "for word."

With regard, finally, to the question whether at the sessions of the *Amphictyons* the art had been prasticed, we know of no recorded passage which could justify such a belief, either in the writings of the ancients or in the monographs of the moderns. The more important resolutions of this council were engraved upon stone tablets, which sometimes were broken by those against whom the resolutions were directed. As this tribunal of the *Amphictyons*, "whose "origin cannot be clearly recognized in the dawn of the early morn-"ing of Greek history, vanishes again unnoticed in that dusk which "shrouds the later evening of Greek history more than that of any "other people," it may not lie entirely beyond the reach of possible facts, that in the later days of the decline of Greece, tachygraphy was occasionally employed at those meetings of the Greeks. If, however, any one is inclined as a friend of "events that might have happened," to entertain this presumption, it would unquestionably be without any value to us, as it refers to a far later period than the one with which we have to do in this chapter.

With regard to the origin of quick-writing among the Romans, Gabelsberger, supported by the words of Isidor : "Common signs were invented—1100—by Ennius," points to the poet Quintus Ennius of Rudiæ, of whom it is said, that he "was as conversant with "the Latin and Greek, as with the Oscan,"-and "had applied him-"self with not a little diligence to the yet uncultivated language of

" the Romans in those days," as the introducer of the art of quick-writing in the Roman state. Anders differs from his predecessor regarding this, inasmuch as he (probably on the ground of an utterance of Sueton) attributes it to Ennius Grammaticus, known " as a translator and language-builder," and not to Ennius, the poet. But apart from that passage in Isidor, the writings of the ancients that have come down to us do not contain any intelligence that attributes such work to the tragic poet and philologist (so often mentioned by Cicero and Quintilian), nor to the younger Ennius mentioned by Sueton. The statement of Isidor is highly inaccurate. This author seems to have published his "*Notices*" without the necessary critique and elaboration. Evidence of this is found, in our opinion, in the very wording of some passages incoherently connected with the sentences immediately following. His "notes" have been explained in radically contradictory ways; hence the criticism of many, that he contradicted himself; and hence Kopp's attempt to refute this criticism as unjustifiable. In consequence of these facts, the statement of Isidor loses considerable in weight. His statement alone is insufficient, especially if we compare it with the words of Plutarch—an author who wrote about 100 A. D., and who, therefore, had a better understanding of the period in question than Isidor—which we have quoted on a previous occasion, when the manner in which Cicero saved a speech of Cato, the younger, was described, namely : " for as yet they had developed neither quick-writers nor did they " have any, but were just entering that path." His statement, moreover, appears insufficient if we consider the quality of Isidor's collection.

As we intend in the next chapter, which is devoted especially to tachygraphy of the Romans, the Tironean Notes, to enter upon the spirit and meaning of the words of Plutarch (quoted there as well as here), we may content ourselves for the present with having stated our conviction, that there cannot be any question as to the non-existence of stenography in Rome before the days of Cicero.

As in the present section we have dealt with unfounded suppositions regarding the age of stenography, we now enter the field of the real history of this art.

ROMAN AND GREEK SHORTHAND.

*Primordia et incrementa, quae ceperit tachygraphia
Romana, si qui nostris temporibus diligenter explicare
incipiunt, ii profecto neque acta agere videntur, neque
in negotio, versari non satis digno eruditorum dili-
gentia.**

Sarpe proleg. ad tachygr. Rom.

Prior to the advent of tachygraphy to Rome, the necessity for
writing faster than usual seems to have led to a mode of abbreviation, based simply upon the principle of designating the most frequently occurring words by an initial letter of the word, or by several
initial letters ; frequently with an addition of the middle letters
which began a syllable, and often, by the addition of one or more
final letters. Marcus Valerius Probus, of Beryt, a famous grammarian who lived under Nero (54–68 A. D.) expressly says, in
his treatise on the abbreviations that had formerly been in use :
" Among the ancients when tachygraphy was not yet practiced,
" those especially, who were present in the Senate, for the purpose
" of writing down that which had been said, designated, for the
" sake of rapidity, certain words and names with initial letters only,
" according to a mutual agreement, and what these several letters
" signified was clearly understood." These abbreviations were called
singulae literae siglae ; and they were the forerunners of genuine
shorthand writing.

The manner in which the most literal reports were made before
the days of tachygraphical help, is expressed in the following words
of Isidor, bishop of Sevilla, who lived in the first third of the seventh
century. He describes it thus : " Whatever was spoken in the assem-
" bly or before the court, was written down at the same time by the
" several writers present, after they had divided amongst themselves
" their respective parts and had agreed on how many words each
" should take down, and in what order." This was exactly the same
procedure which was current under the name of the polygraphic
method, in the earlier days among the Italian quick writers in Turin,
and which has already been fully described by me in another work ;
the same procedure was also employed by the twelve Lords of the
Round-table of Léodey's in taking down the proceedings of the national constitutional and legislative assembly of France in the last
decade of the last century.

Passing from the *siglae* (which for a long time served as a substitute
for tachygraphy, and which, even after shorthand writing had been
invented, was constantly used in public and private life) to the
Roman quick-writing, we are first called upon to solve the question : How did this art arise? We are bound to take a positive

---

*" If any one in our times would attempt to trace the origin of Roman shorthand,
" and set forth its growth, he would not indeed, seem to perform a useless labor nor to
" engage in an undertaking unworthy of the attention of learned men."

stand against the assertion, presented by philologists and historians, " that the Roman quick-writing had formed itself through necessity " and practice and had gradually developed, so that we cannot " properly speak of *the inventor of it.*" The idea of producing a writing which by the re-formation of the usual letters (for the sake of greater facility, as well as for the sake of a better connection) and by employing certain abbreviations according to certain principles to enable the initated to fix the quick speech, has necessarily arisen in a certain person who may have busied himself diligently with the question : In what easier and more perfect manner than by way of the *siglae* can the verbiage of a speech be fixed? and then recognizing the practicability of this idea endeavored to give it a convenient and definite shape. A system like that of the Tironian Notes will never arise of itself. Even in modern times we only know of systems, which, emanating from different and distinct inventors, were usually named after them ;—we know of none, the signs and principles of which had formed themselves through " necessity and practice and gradually become a system." It is similar with the formation of alphabets ; it must be assumed that each must have had a distinct inventor. Whether a certain and sufficient knowledge of the inventor and of the circumstances of his life has come down to us through so many centuries is another question.

By whom, and when, the Roman tachygraphy was invented is difficult to determine, and possibly cannot be satisfactorily decided. But in order to arrive at some fair conclusion, we must consider the statements of the ancients which allude to the origin of a distinct Roman quick-writing.

We have intimated at the close of the last section that we cannot concur in the opinion based upon the authority of Isidor : " Common abbreviations, 1100, were invented first by Ennius," or that Ennius had introduced tachygraphy in Rome. To refute these statements we hardly need subject the credibility of this authority to a closer investigation. Isidor lived in a dark age. When he composed the encyclopedia, edited by him under the name of the Primitive History, he issued it without a clear understanding of the subject—he borrowed his statements, mostly, from the grammarians who flourished from the second to the fourth century and left historical facts almost entirely out of consideration. While these facts alone are apt to weaken his testimony, we, on our part, do not see the slightest ground for the assumption that he thought of tachygraphy when he spoke of the common abbreviations (*vulgares notae*). The " common abbreviations " are no more nor less than the *siglae* which had come early into use among the Romans and were called *vulgares*, because they were employed by everybody. Siglae, therefore, not tachygraphic signs, were invented by Ennius. The ques-

tion whether by this Ennius, is meant the poet Quintus Ennius of
Rudiä (239–169 B. C.), or the grammarian Ennius, of whom Sueton
makes mention (about 120 B. C.), or even a third person of
this name, we are not prepared to answer. One of the most
important historical records which gives us with some degree
of certainty the time in which the art of shorthand writing
came into use at Rome, and which, compared with other testimonies
or proofs, points to the inventor of this art, is the passage in Plutarch
repeatedly quoted by us (Cato, Chap. 23). For a better understanding
of the words of Plutarch we beg leave to present the following :

When Catiline had become convinced through the popular agita-
tion which the first speech of Cicero against him in the senate had
created (delivered on the 8th of November, 63 B. C.) which showed
that his pernicious plans were well known, fearing for his own
personal safety in Rome under Cicero's watchful eyes, he went
with his army to Etruria, leaving the management of his affairs in
Rome to C. Cethegus and P. Lentulus. The conspirators left behind
in the city, as well as other partisans of Catiline, mostly men of
good families, but without any moral character, who sought their
fortune in a total revolution of affairs, despairing at last of the possibility of adding to their number in Rome, turned their attention
to obtaining foreign aid. For this purpose they called on the ambassadors of the Allobrogi (a Gallic people) who had come to complain
of the conduct of Roman officials in their country, and who were
on the eve of leaving the city because their complaints had received
no favorable hearing. At first the Allobrogi readily listened to the
conspirators' proposals, but soon thereafter, reflecting on the conse-
quences and the risks of such enterprises, they communicated everything to Fabius Sanga, their advocate in the city, who, in turn, lost
no time in informing Cicero thereof. Cicero then employed the Allobrogi to make accurate observations of the conspirators' doings. In
this way he succeeded in obtaining written proofs which he placed
unopened before the senate convoked in the Temple of Concord.
From these documents, as well as from the confessions of the conspirators who were seized in Rome, the guilt of the latter became
clearly apparent, and the known participants in the conspiracy were,
by resolution of the senate, given into the custody of various sena-
tors. But when the prisoners, through their aiders and abettors,
sought to incite the populace, and mustered their slaves and freedmen in order to free themselves, forcibly, from custody, Cicero,
three days after the arrest of those partisans of Catiline, again convoked the senate to decide upon the question : what shall be done
with the prisoners who were confessedly guilty of high treason, in
view of the fact that their adherents assumed a menacing attitude?
D. Junius Silanus, consul elect, first took the floor and moved that
the prisoners, as well as some who had escaped arrest by taking
flight, should be sentenced to death. All expressed themselves in

3

the same way except Julius Cæsar, then prætor. He voted for confiscation of the property and life-long imprisonment of the conspirators. This milder sentence seemed to gain ground, when Cato of Utica, taking up, again, the recommendation of Silanus, procured a victory for the harsher sentence by the power of his oratory.

It is this speech of which Plutarch says: "It had been preserved by the well-known instrumentality of Cicero." Sallust only gives the speeches of Cæsar and Cato—quite naturally so—for they were the only important ones.

Those who incline to the opinion that these speeches handed down by Sallust were authentic, or based upon stenographic reports, are mistaken. The ancient historians never preserved stenographic speeches. Sallust, too, evidently edited in his mind these two speeches, as all other speeches that appear in his works, for they all bear the stamp of his own diction. But apart therefrom we may well assume that both Cæsar and Cato, in proceedings of such grave importance, had spoken longer than ten minutes—the time which the speeches quoted by Sallust take up in reciting.

After putting into the proper light the occasion and subject of that speech of Cato, our next task is to consider the words of Plutarch himself, and to weigh what inferences for our purpose may be gleaned from them.

" This speech of Cato," we read, " has been preserved in this man-
" ner: Cicero had taught the most skilful writers, beforehand, signs,
" which in small and short characters comprehended the signification
" of many letters. These writers he placed in different parts of the
" curia, for as yet they had developed neither quick-writers, nor did
" they have any, but were just entering upon that path."

Primarily,—it seems evident that in the words: " signs which in
" small and short characters comprehended the signification of many
" letters," lies a clear and definite allusion to the fact that we have no longer to do with mere *siglae*, for these were not necessarily small and short characters. It is no less significant that we read: $\tau \dot{\upsilon} \pi o \iota$, not $\gamma \rho \dot{\alpha} \mu \mu \alpha \tau \alpha$ or $\sigma \tau o \iota \chi \epsilon \tilde{\imath} \alpha$. Should we not rather infer from this that Plutarch was not thinking of common letters, but of peculiar signs? The remarks of Plutarch would have been idle if he only meant to say that certain words, for the sake of brevity, were expressed with the initial letters, for that was commonly known to every one at the time. He must have had something rather unknown in mind. Even if the Greeks did not comprehend the nature of the Roman tachygraphy, they would certainly have endeavored to faithfully reproduce the exterior form as it appeared to them.

In regard to the mode of obtaining stenographic reports of proceedings in those days, Plutarch observes that " Cicero posted stenographers in various places in the curia." According to this an alternation in the manner, as Isidor describes it, cannot be in question. The employment of several quick-writers was surely for no other purpose than to put together something complete from the several imperfect reports of the entire proceedings by collecting all the notations ; in other words, it was done with a view to meet the, as yet, imperfect development of that new art.

Therefore, about the year 63 B. C. tachygraphy was known and practiced at Rome.

It may be mentioned in this connection that Sarpe assigns even an earlier date for the employment of stenographers. He says " the " second accusation against Verres shows plainly that in the year " 70 B. C. the statements of witnesses were noted down by quick- " writers, for if such had not been employed during the first pro- " ceedings, Cicero could not possibly have had the statements made by " witnesses in the first proceedings, read aloud during the second, " viz., in the first book (49, 128) the evidence of C. Fannius, in the . " second, the statements of M. Cullus, Clorus and Dio, or in the fourth " those of Archagathus and Lentullus. The accusations against " Verres, as is well known, were brought forward in the year 684 of " the city, or 70 before Christ. The supposition that those who " wrote down the words in the courts made use of *siglae* merely is, " as every one sees, opposed by the fact that as there were *siglae* but " for very few words and sentences, these would not have answered " the required purpose. Valerius Probus, too, to whom a book on " the notes (that is, *siglae*) is ascribed, knows nothing of the use of " the *siglae* for reporting court proceedings." Apart from the fact that Sarpe seems to have forgotten that the words of Valerius Probus, to which he alludes, reading thus : " *Maxime in senatu qui scribendo aderant*" (those who were present in the senate for the purpose of writing) do not necessarily exclude the employment of the *siglae* ; again, that in the passage of Isidor, largely commented on by Sarpe himself, it is expressly stated : " The employment of these abbrevia- " tions (the *siglae*) took place in such a manner that all which was " spoken in the assemblage or before the tribunal, etc," the opinion of Sarpe seems to be completely unfounded, because, otherwise, stenography, at that time, must have been very extensively em- ployed over the whole Roman Empire if it was already used in the Sicilian tribunals for the purpose of recording, although it had not then even been employed in the Roman senate.

It is indisputable that these momentous proceedings of the senate alluded to, affecting the whole empire, gave the impulse to the in- vention and propagation of shorthand writing. In Greece, in con- sequence of the small extent of the States, the words of the orator could reach the ears of all the citizens of the respective States and a stenographic report, for this very reason, was scarcely a necessity.

In Rome, on the contrary, it was essential to produce a verbatim report in order to cause the debates, proceedings, and weighty resolutions to re-echo through the vast empire. So much the more they must have felt themselves impelled thereto, as the eyes of all who sojourned in the provinces were directed to the metropolis and every one wished to be informed as accurately as possible on the important proceedings that took place there.

If we now turn to the question : " Who may be considered the inventor of Roman tachygraphy, we must, at the outset, refute the opinion to which Plutarch's words : " Cicero had taught those skilled writers tachygraphy," might give rise, and which seem already to have given rise to the opinion that this celebrated orator and statesman of Rome had invented Roman shorthand writing. Contrary hereto we must bear in mind the fact that in the days of antiquity the merits of the freedmen were but too frequently ascribed to their patrons (in some respects in analogy with the accepted maxim that whatever a slave acquired, he acquired not for himself, but for his master), and that accordingly Plutarch may easily have ascribed to Cicero what (as we shall show further on) belonged to Tiro. We ought, furthermore, to consider that the slaves and freedmen at Rome rendered the greatest service to the literary world as copyists, readers, stenographers, and in many other ways. The book trade, for instance, was almost exclusively in the hands of freedmen. We must be mindful of the words of Seneca ; "that all these things, the stenographic signs, were only inventions of the lowest slaves," which show that stenography was no fashionable branch, to the study of which the aristocratic Romans condescended. We must further consider that Cicero, had he been the inventor or merely the perfecter of shorthand writing, would not have remained silent about it, if we are to judge from his whole character and nature ; and that even in the writings of his biographers and commentators no allusion whatever to such a meritorious achievement can be found.

In regard to the words of Cicero : " what I wrote to you about the "ten ambassadors, I believe you have not properly understood be- "cause I wrote to you by means of signs,"—on which words the opposition to the opinion given in the above paragraph is based, the expression, διὰ σημείων furnishes no clue to what these signs were ; whether they were brief or secret signs. Most probably the latter signs were meant, as Cicero would surely not have written part of his letter in a new kind of writing from the mere vanity of employing new signs ; far more likely, he did it in order to communicate to his friends, by means of secret signs, important intelligence which was intended solely for Atticus and not for others into whose hands the letter might accidentally fall. Whilst Roman citizens generally did not busy themselves with tachygraphy, we know that they not infrequently made use of the *latebra scribendi*. Aulus Gellius tells us in his Attic Nights, amongst other things, that Cæsar, in his correspondence with C. Oppius and Balbus Cornelius, designated each letter by another sound than the one generally used; and Sueton reports that the secret writing of Augustus consisted in making the second letter of the alphabet the first, the third the second, etc., and that he designated the last letter by *aa*. Finally, a passage in Cassius Dio (xl., 9) may be mentioned here, in which we read of a report forwarded by a legate of Cicero relating to a communication from Cæsar saying : "For fear that his "instructions should fall into hands for whom they were not in-"tended, he made use of a perverted mode of writing which could "not be understood by any one but the one for whom it was in-"tended."

To Cicero, therefore, is not due the merit of the invention or even of the development of Roman shorthand writing. But that he furthered this art to the best of his ability, on account of the advantages it offered to himself, we may well believe.

On the other hand his freedman, Tiro, named after him 54 B. C., seems justly to be entitled to the name of inventor of Roman tachygraphy. Eusebius (325 A. D.) or Hieronymous (373 A. D.) says : "Marcus Tullius Tiro, the freedman of Cicero, who first invented the stenographic signs, etc." A confirmation of this statement is found in the words of Isidor : "In Rome, Tullius, the freedman "of Cicero, first elucidated stenographic signs, but only for "the prepositions." That Tiro, above all others, possessed great skill in quick-writing is shown in the letters of his master to Atticus. We read there : "But I have by no means "dictated to Tiro, who is accustomed to follow entire periods, but "I have dictated by syllables to Spintharus." If we remember the passage in Plutarch, discussed at length above, in which he evidently ascribes to the master what is due to the servant, and bear in mind the words of Seneca, who calls stenography an invention of the slaves ; and if we finally put together all the facts presented, we certainly find the strongest probability that the much disputed statement that Tiro, the talented freedman of the great Roman statesman and orator, invented and developed the stenographic art, is the correct one, an opinion which is also supported by Sickel's argument against Kopp (commentaries on the documents of the first Carlovingians p. 327).

From the words of Isidor just alluded to, it further appears (that is, supposing we read *commentatus* and not *commentus*) that Tiro had written a sort of compendium of tachygraphy. It is true we find neither in Gellius nor in Asconius, who speak of the literary activity of that freedman, a positive and direct allusion to such a work. It, however, may be assumed that such a work had formed part of the

" Pandects " of Tiro mentioned by Gellius. This statement of Isidor finds again some confirmation in the words of the Abbot Trithemius : " That Marcus Tullius Cicero, the eloquent Roman, had composed a rather extensive work on tachygraphy," when we remember that, as a rule, (as we have shown before), what was due to the servant was ascribed to the master. We shall later have an opportunity to refer again to this collection of notes.

Noteworthy is an utterance of Fossé, regarding the services of stenographers at that time. He says : " *Il est fort douteux que les séméiographes fussent parvenus à une très-grande accélération. Ils suivaient la parole des orateurs, voilà un fait incontestable ; mais s' il est vrai, comme le dit Quinctilian dans son Traité du geste, que Cicéron mettait jusqu'à trois heures à prononcer ses discours, nous devons en conclure, que l'art n'était pas alors aussi difficile que de notre temps. Les orateurs anciens parlaient sur des places publiques, en présence de toute une cité : pour se faire entendre il leur fallait enfler la voix, et l'émission des mots en était d'autant ralentie. La rapidité du discours est en raison inverse de l'espace dans lequel il est prononcé.*"[*]

If we now ask : what men besides Tiro are named who made themselves conspicuous as Roman shorthand writers, we first meet the following often quoted passages in Isidor : The next was Vipsanius Philargyrus, a freedman of M. Vipsanius Agrippa, (died 13 B. C.). Next Isidor mentions Aquila, a freedman of C. Cilnius Maecenas, (died 8 B. C.). Here, also, the fact is repeated that to Maecenas is ascribed what his freedman had done. Dio Cassius (155–229 A. D.) gives in his history, after relating the death of Maecenas, a description of the manifold merits of this man. He states what wholesome influence he had exerted upon Augustus ; that he had been the first to introduce warm baths at Rome, and then adds, that he "likewise had first invented shorthand writing signs " and had the same taught to many others by his freedman, Aquilla." It is by no means to be supposed that Maecenas himself had a hand in the development of Roman shorthand writing, as might be inferred from Dio's words.

Even Lipsius doubts this. Still less, according to what we have before shown, is the opinion well-founded that this statesman laid the foundation of Roman tachygraphy. This needs no further refutation. Perhaps Dio merely meant to say that Maecenas, that is, his freedman, Aquilla, invented some signs and made use of them. Although it may be regarded as tolerably certain that Maecenas, no

---

[*] " It is very doubtful whether the semiographers had attained very great swiftness. " That they followed the words of the orators—is an incontestable fact, but, if it is true, as "Quintilian says in his treatise on Gesture that Cicero consumed as much as three " hours in delivering his speeches, we must conclude therefrom that the stenographic " art was not as difficult to master in those days as in our times. The ancient orators "spoke in public places in the presence of a whole city ; in order to make themselves " heard, they were obliged to inflate their voices and the utterance of their words was, "consequently, somewhat slackened. The rapidity of speech is in inverse ratio to the " time of deliverance.'

more than Cicero and Vipsanius Agrippa, had learned and practiced, and that these distinguished Romans had rather called this art into their service, yet there is no doubt that that minister of Augustus (Maecenas) rendered another service to shorthand which may be more highly estimated than that of augmenting the number of stenographic signs. From Dio's communication we may infer that Maecenas, appreciating the advantage and significance of tachygraphy, exerted his influence to have this art taught, and perhaps made its teaching compulsory by the state, with a view of making it serviceable for public purposes. This inference would gain more credibility if the statement made by Gabelsberger (Anleitung z. d. Redez-Kunst-München, 1834, S. 45.) was based on fact, the authority for which we have vainly sought, namely : "That "during the life of Augustus there were about 300 special schools "in the Roman Empire in which nothing but stenography was "taught."

With regard to "Seneca," mentioned by Isidor as a promoter and developer of Roman shorthand writing, opinions are greatly divided as to whether it means, M. Annäus Seneca, the orator (56 B. C. 34 A. D.), or his son Lucius Annäus Seneca, the philosopher (3–65 A. D.). Lipsius and Kopp decide for the former. Sarpe, on the other hand, is of the opposite opinion. He takes the ground that : "even if Lucius expressed himself contemptuously with regard to tachy graphy, he only did so, when in opposition to Posidonius (of Agamea, called the Rhodian, a philosopher and historian, who lived from 135 to 51 B. C., and whose writings have only come down to us in fragments, so that we do not know against which passage and which of his works the attack of Seneca was directed) he denied that philosophy was the mother of the arts of every day life, and that we were indebted to the ingenuity of man to devise the arts and not to his wisdom. Wisdom is seated deeper ; it does not make the hand skilled in arts ; it is the ruler of thought. But if we would infer from this that Seneca despised in life what he denied in his writings, one might as well go so far as to deny him eloquence, learning, ambition and the possession of unlimited wealth. But as Lucius himself had written much, and in part, as his writings show, had frequently dictated, what prevents us from assuming that shorthand writing had interested him sufficiently to induce him to collect and make additions to the stenographic signs? In addition to this we must bear in mind that it was customary with the Latin authors to designate well-known men only by one name, less known ones, by several. But if, in spite of this, we should incline to the opinion that Seneca himself had nothing to do with the collection of tachygraphic signs, we must remember that in Greek and Latin it is frequently said of a person that he had done *this* or *that*—which had been done only by his order or by some representative."

Here again we see entirely different opinions opposed to each other. No wonder, for all facts relating to the tachygraphy of the ancients are more or less shrouded in obscurity and it would be difficult, if not impossible, to present the truth in every instance. If we are called upon to state our opinion we will express the conviction that neither the orator nor the philosopher took the trouble to learn stenography, far less to enrich it with new inventions. Such an occupation of either, is, in our opinion, diametrically opposed to the known direction of their minds. The works of the father as the works of the son, especially the latter, are characterized by deterioration. At that time, we find, profound knowledge was no longer the main thing. Troublesome and time-exhausting special researches entering into details were already looked down upon with a certain degree of superciliousness, just as in our time able and detailed studies are disposed of by certain writers simply designating them as pedantic. Not considering that great and general results are the fruits only of unceasing and earnest investigation, they expected to reap the harvest without taking the trouble to bestow their undivided attention to the tree which was to bear the fruit. We cannot wonder that the fruit gathered was poor. The writings of the courtier, and so-called philosopher, Seneca, are of a flimsy, fastidious character. The ideas express that tone of aristocracy which, by the way, the sentence : " stenography was an invention of the meanest race of slaves" strikingly illustrates. How can we then suppose that such authors would have busied themselves with an occupation "so dry and lusterless" as the collection of tachygraphic signs and their augmentation ? If the rhetorician, or his son, had really condescended to do such work, surely neither of them would have put his " light under a bushel ;" at least not the latter, whose well-known vanity would surely not have allowed such an achievement to sink into oblivion. Nowhere in his numerous letters and dissertations do we find the least allusion to the matter. Again, the ground which Sarpe assumes for his supposition that widely-known men were briefly designated by one name only, is by no means reliable. Frequently unimportant men were designated only by one name, as for instance, Ennius, the grammarian, while there existed a famous poet of that name, hence a distinction of the latter from the former would have appeared to be a necessity. On the other hand, celebrated men were not infrequently designated by several names, as Marcus Tullius Cicero.

There was, besides, another Seneca who lived, at the latest, about the time of Domitian in the first century after Christ, and who edited the poems of Lucan ; this Seneca might be the one alluded to. Nay, if we consider that the name of Seneca was by no means an uncommon one, even a third supposition would not appear out of place. This supposition is, that shortly after Tiro, Philargyrus and Aquila in their noble strife to bring Roman shorthand writing to blooming perfection in the circles accessible to them (the circle of the copyists and grammarians) had laid a firm foundation, a freedman by the name of Seneca gathered much of the scattered materials and augmented them by his own additional devices.

. "Everywhere," says Schmitz, in his Tironiana, "the name of Seneca!" Which Seneca is meant? While the claims of Tiro to an essential share in the invention and·development of Roman stenography are not disputed by any one, it is impossible, from the nature of our traditions, to give a definite answer to the query about who was the particular Seneca alluded to by Schmitz. I forego, therefore, a discussion of the various hypotheses which declare in favor of the rhetorician or the philosopher, or against father and son, and in favor of a third person of that name. Only the following two remarks I would offer concerning the activity of that mysterious personage. First, Krause errs when he says that Seneca's "work contained about 15,000 stenographic signs, as we glean from a work of Isidor," for in Gruter we find, including the numerous Christian notes, altogether only about 13,000—compare Kopp 1, paragraph 71, page 57. Second, Sarpe already says in his Prolegg. ad Tachygr. Rome, page 26 (compare Zeibig page 30) with full justice, although not with the desirable emphasis, that the frequently quoted words in the 90th letter of the philosopher Seneca (paragraph 25), "*quid verborum notas . . . vilissimorum mancipiorum ista commenta sunt,*" do not by any means compel us to claim for their author a share in the origination of the collection of notes.

It is necessary now to enter briefly, but more accurately than hitherto upon the train of thoughts. After Seneca had, on the one hand, declared himself, in consonance with Posidonius' philosophy, that philosophy was the author of a happy life and the ruler of the golden age, he, on the other hand, opposed the opinion of that philosopher (Posidonius), that philosophy was the source of invention of the arts of every day life, and asserts that philosophy had no more to do with the art of building houses and cities than in laying out our artificial fish ponds ; all these things, he maintained, emanated from desire of luxury as did " ferramenta fabrilia," and the working of metal generally . . . (§19) " a natura luxuria descivit, quae . . . novissime animum corpori addixit [the extravagance, which very recently sacrificed the soul to the body,—the substance to the form—was a departure from nature."] The assertion of Posidonius (§20), " omnia " haec sapiens quidem invenit : sed minora quam ut ipse tractaret, " sordidioribus ministris dedit" was also wrong : " immo non aliis " excogitata ista sunt quam quibus hodieque curantur : quaedam " nostra demum prodisse memoria scimus, ut speculariorum usum " perlucente testa clarum transmittentium lumen, ut suspensuras

4

" balneorum et impressos parietibus tubos per quos circumfunderetur
" calor, qui ima simul ac summa foveret aequaliter . . . quid loquar
" marmora, quibus templa, quibus domus fulgent ? quid lapideas
" moles in rotundum ac leve formatas, quibus porticus et capacia
" populorum tecta suscipimus ? *quid verborum notas, quibus quamvis*
" *citata excipitur oratio et celeritatem linguae manus sequitur? vilis-*
" *simorum mancipiorum ista commenta sunt. Sapientia altius sedet*
" *nec manus edocet : animorum magistra est.*"*

Who does not see that in this connection not merely the " verborum notae," but also other previously mentioned artificialities
(" quaedam nostra demum . . . tecta suscipimus ")are included in
the meaning of " commenta?" If this be the case, who can prove
that those " commenta" had all emanated from real slaves,
who, in consequence of their condition, were lightly esteemed ? If
such proof could be given, we should nevertheless be compelled to
admit that Seneca did not refer to the generally despised caste of
slaves, but to the sentiment which instigated these inventions. In
other words, by the " vilissima mancipia" we must not understand,
contemptible slaves in the civic sense, but men, who, contrary to the
higher aspiration and the nobler activity of the " sage" aiming at
the elevation of mind, had been estranged from natural simplicity
and became slaves to their artificially increased wants, by showing
a servile sentiment in the creation and satisfaction of these wants, in
opposition to the higher aims of wisdom.

The question who the " Seneca" was that Isidor mentions will
hardly ever be answered satisfactorily. We know next to nothing
about the life and activity of the ancient Roman grammarians, apart
from Sueton's little work. The reason for this seems simply to be
that these grammarians were considered too insignificant to have
the circumstances of their lives handed down to posterity. Whoever
that Seneca may have been, this much may be regarded as certain,
that his collection had for its object especially to promote a certain
uniformity in the method of writing and abbreviation among all the
shorthand writers ; for even at that time occasional important differences and peculiarities of prominent shorthand writers appeared.
In the following statements and references we shall not separate the

*[" A wise man indeed invented (or discovered) all these things; but matters that
" were too trivial for him to discuss he left to humbler instruments. Nay, indeed,
" these very things were thought out by other than those by whom they are cultivated
" at the present time; finally we know that certain things have been discovered within
" our own memory, as for example, the use of mirrors for the transmission of bright
" light: the arching (or vaulting) of baths and the insertion of tubes in walls of houses
" by means of which warmth is diffused, so that the lowest and highest parts are equally
" warmed. Why should I mention the marble with which temples and houses are
" adorned ? Why the masses of stone moulded into gracefully rounded columns with
" which we support porticos and spacious dwelling houses?" Again, " Why the signs
" of words, with which a speech though rapid, is taken down and the hand follows (or
" keeps up with) the speed of the tongue ? These are the inventions (devices or con-
" trivances) of men in a servile station (or men of servile occupations). Wisdom holds
" a loftier place, and does not instruct the hands. It is the sovereign (literally, *mistress*)
" of the intellect."]

Greek tachygraphy from the Roman, to avoid too many details in our exposition.

It is hardly necessary to prove that Tiro and his associates communicated shorthand writing to others. We have, moreover, already intimated that Maecenas encouraged instruction in this art. It is also generally assumed that Cæsar Augustus instructed his grandsons in stenography, an assumption based upon the words of Sueton (Nepotes et literas et notare aliaque rudimenta per se plerumque docuit.) taking for granted, that Lipsius means in that passage : *notare—notas intelligere—*; instead of the earlier expression reading *natare*. To be sure, Torrentius, in opposition to this, and as we believe justly, asserts that the expression "literas et natare" like the Greek "*μήτε νεῖν μήτε γράμματα*" had been a universally known and current phrase to designate the harmonius cultivation of the child which does not permit the body to be neglected for the intellect. The object of Augustus was to develop his grandsons, who were some time to become the rulers of a great empire, into competent men endowed with intellectual and bodily vigor of the highest order.

Still more definite evidence of the fact that shorthand writing was an object of instruction, especially of juveniles, we find in an edict issued by the Emperor Diocletian, A. D. 301, concerning the highest prizes and rewards for bodily and mental development. We read there that the teacher of shorthand writing should receive 75 Denares per month for every pupil. This passage gives us, at the same time, an intimation of the salary paid to the then teachers of tachygraphy. From Mommsen's investigations regarding the value of the Denare adopted as standard measure by Diocletian, we conclude that the 75 Denares mentioned there amounted to about $1.30. If, therefore, such a teacher had a large number of pupils we may figure out a profitable sum for him as monthly salary. For the sake of comparison, we beg leave to state that for instruction in reading and writing for each individual boy, 50 Denares (about $1) was paid monthly, but for intruction in the Latin and Greek languages 200 Denares were paid.

From communications left by the poet Prudentius (born about 348 A. D. at Calahorra in Spain) we learn that after having been expelled from his Episcopal see at Brescia, the holy Cassianus, in the fourth century, established a school at Imola and instructed juveniles, among other things, in shorthand writing ; but finally he was killed by his exasperated pupils with their styluses.

Further corroboration of the fact that the art of shorthand writing constituted a part of juvenile instruction, we find in the words of the grammarian, F. Planciades Fulgentius, (480 A. D.) "all instruction "is of a lower and higher nature, as the instruction of the youth in "writing, is divided in the usual one, and the stenographic one."

Finally, Theodoretos, bishop of Kyrrhas in Syria (386–458), relates in his ecclesiastical history of a certain Protogenes, who being banished to the city of Antinous, likewise established a school and instructed his pupils in shorthand writing, as well as in religion.

Before we pass to an exhibit of the variety of shorthand writing employed in the days prior to Cicero, down to the Church fathers, permit me to refer to the fact that writing, after the invention of shorthand writing proper, had become threefold: First, a writing of all the letters of the word, *perscribere*, which included the caligraphy; γράφειν εἰς κάλλος; second, a writing in *siglae*, and third, a writing in tachygraphic signs, *notis* or *per compendia scribere*. The stenographers were called σημειογράφει, ταχυγράφοι, ὀξυγράφοι, γραμματεῖς, ὑπογραφεῖς, ὑπογραμματεῖς, ὑποδεχεῖς, νοτάριοι, *notarii*, *actuarii*, *exceptores*, etc., but if we would infer that these words always, and under all circumstances, meant shorthand writers in our sense of the word, we should frequently err, for their meaning is very uncertain. There is no help for it—we are compelled in each case to investigate the context of the sentence to get at the proper designation We may, however, omit to dwell at large on the name of this art, and its disciples, for the reason that the following facts throw sufficient light on this question to make it clear.

A further interpolation which we may be permitted to make, is the following: Sueton relates of the Emperor Titus (79–81) that he often in pleasantry, for a wager, vied with a writer in tachygraphy, and the bishop of Ptolemais, Synesios (378–430) mentions in his 61st letter a shorthand writer by the name of Asterios to whom he had promised a large Egyptian carpet. The accurate description which Synesios gives of Asterios was caused by apprehension that the present might fall into the hands of another person of the same name and profession, which proves that neither the name nor the vocation of the person named was an uncommon one.

If we ask of what use was stenography to the ancients, we find that this art was a servant of public, political, judicial, ecclesiastical and scientific oratory; it was an auxiliary to authors and statesmen in their studies, in fact, it was employed in the most varied manner, which will move us to dwell further upon passages in the writings of the ancients tending to prove this.

Sueton says in his life of Julius Cæsar that there were some speeches erroneously ascribed to him, for instance the oration for Q. Metellus, which Augustus, not without reason, thought had not been edited by himself, but by shorthand writers who were not able to follow the words of the orator properly. It may not be irrelevant to quote briefly what Sarpe says concerning this oration of Cæsar. As this oration, in which Julius defends Metellus as well as himself against the accusations of the common accusers, seems to have been delivered in the year after the discovery of the Catilinian conspiracy, that is in the year 62 B. C., at which time there had been no shorthand writers as yet employed in the senate to report the proceedings, and as we nowhere read that proceedings had been instituted against Q. Metellus in the forum on the charge of having, by his laws, disturbed the peace of the state, the inference is justifiable that this oration was delivered in the *Comitiae* in which Julius (according to the report of Sueton—Julius 16) put himself forward in opposition to the people's tribune, as defender of Metellus, who had decreed peace-disturbing laws against the will of his colleagues. It might therefore be inferred that (as Sueton reports) after Cæsar had become consul he ordered "to take down and to publish, not only the proceedings of the "senate, but also those of the people." Hence the employment of shorthand writing in the *Comitiae* in the year 54 B. C.

Q. Asconius Pedianus remarks in his commentary on the oration of Cicero for Milo (delivered 52 B. C.), that this oration yet existed in stenographic manuscript, but that it was entirely different from the one which he explained and which justly might be con sidered as one of the most perfect speeches of the time. When Cicero commenced this oration he had been received with clamor by the adherents of Clodius, who were not even to be repressed through fear of the guardians ; he could not, therefore, speak with the firm- ness that otherwise characterized him. Milo himself observes in a witticism, that if Cicero had delivered his speech in the form in which it subsequently came to publicity, he, Milo, would surely not have been compelled to breakfast on as many barbs in his exile as was the case.

M. Fabius Quintilianus of Calahorre (35–95) brought forward in his " Guide to the Art of Oratory," a number of prosecuting speeches circulated under his name, which, in consequence of the carelessness of greedy shorthand writers anxious to earn money, rendered his words faithfully only in a small degree. The same author relates further on in the preface to his above named work, that two books on rhetoric circulated under his name, were neither edited nor even elaborated by him for publication. Both of these works had been written down and published by hearers.

In the satire ascribed to the young Seneca, " The turning into a pumpkin of the Emperor Claudius " it is said that Janus, in the council of the gods, had eloquently said many things which the shorthand writer was not able to follow, and that therefore no re- port was made of them, rather than to express in other words what he had spoken.

Pliny, the younger, (62–113) relates of the elder of this name (23–79) that he constantly had a shorthand writer at his side, even when traveling, and of himself, that he too at times made use of a shorthand writer. A not entirely unimportant passage relating to the age of the invention of Greek tachygraphy might be found in the letters of Flavius Philostratos of Lemnos (195 A. D.) He went from Antioch with two slaves, a shorthand writer and a copyist. A further written evidence regarding a stenographer is found in Böckh, in Corp. inscript. graec. III, page 26, no: 3902 d.

In the celebrated physician Galeno's (131-200) work "On the books that emanated from him," we read, that, one day when he had spoken in public on the works of the ancient physicians he had taken occasion, in that part of the work of Erasistratos on hemorrhage in which bleeding was disproved, to bring forward many things against this colleague of his, with the intention of vexing another physician by the name of Martialis, who called himself a disciple of Erasistratos. After his oration had been applauded he was requested by a friend to dictate what he had spoken to a shorthand writer, in order that he, after his return home, might communicate it to Martialis. The circumstance that Galeno after his return to Rome had seen this speech (which, as he himself confesses, had originated in party zeal) in the hands of many caused him to make the resolution never again to speak in public.

It is evidently this passage to which the Arabian, Mustafa Ben Abdallah Katib Jelebi, usually named Haji Khalfa, alludes in his mention of Roman shorthand writing. Only he does not seem to have had the text before him, but merely reported from memory.

To the Christian church, as we shall show in the following remarks, tachygraphy was of essential service.

At first the shorthand writers used to note down on their own account, what concerned the vicissitudes, utterances and deaths of the highly celebrated martyrs of the church, but subsequently, probably from the beginning of the third century, they acted as official shorthand writers (*notarii ecclesiastici*). Under the reign of Decius, *ecclesiastices* are said to have been appointed by the Roman Bishop Fabian to note down the history of the sufferings of the martyrs.

These martyrs' acts and martyrologies were conducted independently of the acts of the examining judges and the Christians were able often to procure them, by bribing the judicial shorthand writers, or their servants. The martyrs' acts and martyrologies were collected and preserved in the church archives, and publicly read at the martyrs' anniversaries in order thereby to recall the lives, sufferings and death of these men.

TRACEABLE HISTORY OF THE ART.

A certain Aucharus (according to others, Eucharius or Varus) is said to have witnessed the proceedings against Saint Theodoret, and to have been an attentive witness of all the tortures to which those martyrs were subjected, until, overcome with sympathy for their sufferings, he threw away the writing tablets and cast himself at the feet of the Saint. Genesius, of Arles, likewise showed his disdain, and refused to assist at so horrible a scene. The saints Neon and Turbon were also stenographers. So was a deacon by the name of Cornelius. Finally, Siegel mentions still another, a notary, also mentioned by Tertullian, who was tormented by evil spirits.

It has already been intimated, when speaking of the persecutions of the Christians, that shorthand was employed in the law courts, and we meet with a convincing allusion to the same practice in the writings of Eunapius concerning the life of the sophists.

Pröaresius, of Cäsarea, in Cappadocia, (276–368 A. D.) succeeded his instructor in the office of teacher at Athens, and secured, through his extraordinary eloquence, so many scholars that his adherents outnumbered those of all the other sophists, in consequence of which a bitter feeling sprang up between his disciples and those of the other teachers, so that the Prætor found himself compelled to banish Pröaresius from the city. The successor in the prætorship, however, recalled the exiled man, and the latter, immediately on returning to Athens, delivered such a brilliant lecture that the assembled multitude were carried away with enthusiasm. It was on this occasion that the orator requested that shorthand writers, who daily reported the words of the Themis, should be assigned to him, that they might record his entire speech. The shorthand writers were, with great difficulty, able to follow the words of the orator. To excite the still greater admiration of the Athenians, he turned to the stenographers and demanded of them to minutely observe whether he still accurately remembered what he had said, and he then repeated the whole speech without the least error.

That tachygraphers, *exceptores*, officiated as public officers in court proceedings is conclusively shown by the passages from the Pandects cited below. Besides, Damaskios alludes, in the life of Isidor, to this practice. We refer to the passage in the Pandects to show that even wills were written in shorthand. If Gabelsberger interprets from the passage in Am. Marcellinus: "Notaries stood there who immedi- "ately communicated to Cæsar whatever was asked and answered," that tachygraphers are identical with notaries in translation, he is clearly contradicted by Valesius, a commentator of the Roman authors, who, in a foot note upon the above quoted words, expressly states a distinction between *notarii* and *exceptores*, and only recognizes tachygraphers in the latter word.

The story related by Am. Marcellinus, in the details of which it is stated that the wife of a general named Barbatio, called Assyria, caused her female slave, who was familiar with sign-writing (*notarum perita*), to write a letter to her husband, is but a weak argument for the supposition that stenography was extensively employed at the time, as it is not evident from the passage quoted whether a real stenography or only a secret writing was meant.

Again reverting to our statements concerning the early employment of shorthand writing in the Christian era, we must remember that very early in that era it was customary to have the speeches of the first ecclesiastical teachers reported by tachygraphers. We read in Origen (185–254 A. D.) that after he had passed his sixtieth year, and had acquired great skill in speaking, he permitted shorthand writers to report his speeches, a practice which he had not previously allowed.

He dictated his critical exegetical studies concerning the Bible to seven or more shorthand writers, who intermittently changed with each other, which dictations were afterwards given to calygraphers (some of whom were girls) to be written out. The majority of his homilies have been preserved to us through copies made by others, as he was not accustomed to write them himself.

So with Gregory, Bishop of Nazianz, (318–390) in his 32nd discourse, in which he bids farewell to his congregation at Constantinople, and expressly mentions shorthand writers, who, openly or secretly reported his words. Augusti interprets the words $\varphi\alpha\nu\varepsilon\rho\alpha i$ and $\gamma\alpha\nu\delta\dot\alpha\nu o\nu\sigma\alpha\iota$ used on this occasion so that by the former tachygraphers were meant, who wrote down with Gregory's previous knowledge, and who, therefore, were a kind of official writers, but that by the latter tachygraphers were meant, who wrote without his permission, and who perhaps had been secretly sent by his adversaries in order to secure something by which they could accuse him. Likewise, several zealous scholars tachygraphically reported what the apostolic father Cyrillus, Bishop of Jerusalem, (died 386 A. D.) delivered concerning the fundamental doctrines and mysteries of Christianity.

Socrates relates that the sensible and practical sermons of John Chrysostom, presbyter at Athens, (347–407 A. D.) were partly published by himself and partly reported by shorthand writers, which latter fact is positively confirmed by Nikephoros and Georgius Patriarcha. Concerning Atticus, Bishop of Constantinople, the second successor of John, it is said, according to our authorities, that his sermons were so ordinary that they were not deemed worthy of being reported.

The esteem in which Gaudentius, of Brescia, (died 410 A. D.) Bishop of Sebusa, was held is, among other things, made apparent by the fact that many of his sermons were taken down by tachygraphers. But Gaudentius did not look with favor on the stenographers, as he did not consider their reports of his sermons true pictures of his words. He feared his enemies would take advantage of the custom of writing down the sermons and ascribe to him sermons which would cause him to be suspected of heresy. "Gaudentius really had," says Augusti, "every reason to be on his guard, as he was violently per-"secuted by the Arians, and his sermons were frequently falsified "and misrepresented." Sometimes he yielded to the entreaties of his friends to review and correct his reported sermons.

It is related of the apostolic father, Aurelius Augustinus, (354–430 A. D.) that his sermons, which were attended by a great number of heretics, were stenographed whenever occasion offered. This is also indicated by his own words.

A sermon delivered by Archbishop Eusebius, of Alexandria, an influential and powerful clergyman, who probably lived in Justinian's time, is in existence in two forms—a lengthy one and an abbreviated one. That the short one is not an epitome of the longer one is evident, for it contains passages which are not found in the longer. It is very probable that these two forms represent two reports of this sermon, which were written down by different shorthand writers.

Gregory, the Great, (Pope from 590–604) observes in the dedication to Bishop Maximus of his homilies on the Prophet Ezekiel, that he had reviewed and corrected these sermons, which had been taken down by tachygraphers.

"Again," Neander says, " the publication of the records in the ec-"clesiastical proceedings (gesta ecclesiastica), which were taken down "with great accuracy, made necessary the appointment of secre-"taries from the clergy (notarii, exceptores), who were skilled in "rapid writing with abbreviations." The pleadings and important proceedings at the Councils, and especially the discussions concerning dogmatical subjects between the true believers and heretics, had to be reported in shorthand. Eusebius relates, for instance, that a discussion between a certain Malchion and Paulus, of Somosata, was faithfully reported by shorthand writers, and Socrates relates the same of a religious contest of Basilius Ancyranus with Photinus.

We find further the following proofs that the "Tironean Notes" were employed in the Councils—the church gatherings. The records of the great conference held at Carthage on the 2nd of June, 411, confirm the fact that the Donatists obtained the publication of the preceding conference, the proceedings of which were stenographed. St. Augustin relates, in his 141st letter, that eight stenographers, two writing alternately, reported the speeches of the Bishops assembled in Carthage. We also read, in his 44th letter, that, as the notaries were not willing to stenograph any one of his speeches, his faithful adherents themselves took the trouble to do it, which goes to show that shorthand writing was very prevalent.

Hefele, in his history of the Councils, gives a further instance of the employment of notaries to report their proceedings. Clerical

5

men, he says, especially deacons, were used as secretaries, notaries, &c., in the synods; thus, for instance, in Chalcedon the notaries, and particularly their chief, *Primicerius notariorum*, had considerable influence, although they were not entitled to vote. Some of these notaries were official, and served the Synod itself, but every individual Bishop could bring his own notary, and through him could record the proceedings of the sessions, excepting at the Robber's Synod, where the tyrannical Dioskurus allowed only his own notaries and those of his friends to be present.

"In some churches young men who were to be educated for the
"ministerial services were chosen for such tachygraphical purposes,
"as, for instance, to the office of reader. Epiphanius, subsequently
"Bishop of Ticinum (Pavia), in the 5th century, became 'lector'
"when he was eight years old, and, as soon as he had acquired
"practice in the use of abbreviations, he was received among the
"*exceptores* of the church."

"The notaries occupied similar positions to the *Apocrisiarien*
"(that is, deputies who acted in the name of others, especially for
"high church officials), as do our secretaries of legations."

"Furthermore, the Bishops and Patriarchs, on their official jour-
"neys, used shorthand writers as secretaries."

"In Rome, in the 6th century, there were twelve *notarios regio-*
"*narios*, each of whom, in his district (*regio*), performed the duties of
"a notary in ordinary affairs and business, in judicial and non-judi-
"cial proceedings, and regarding donations and grants. Here was also
"the *Primicerius notariorum*, who was afterwards called *Protono-*
"*tarius*, (a title which Gregory had already known), and corre-
"sponded to the *Πρῶτος τῶν πατριαρχικῶν νοταρίων* at Constanti-
"nople, a man of rank and influence. The notaries were, especially
"in ancient times, occasionally called *chartularii*, or *χαρτογράφοι*,
"as well as *χαρτοφύλακες*. In Constantinople, *μέγας χαρτοφύλαξ*
"was a great dignitary, equal to Secretary of State, while the other,
"*χαρτοφύλακες*, corresponded to the ordinary secretaries." In our
opinion, it appears from the above that notaries already at that
time bore rather the character of attorneys-at-law, or such as were
skilled in the interpretation of law, than that of shorthand writers.
Tachygraphy was certainly of great importance to them in
these transactions, although this fact does not appear promi-
nently. This furnishes considerable evidence that tachygraphy
proved of great service to the representatives of the Christian church,
in the publication of their works, in the copying of books, and in
letter writing, &c.

Epiphanius speaks in high terms of one of his scholars, who, with
great care, wrote down in shorthand signs his work concerning the

heresies; and again, of another, Hypatios, who carefully transcribed it from the tablets.

Basilius, the Great, (328–379 A. D.), likewise refers to tachygraphy. In a letter to a shorthand writer, he says: "Words have wings; "therefore we use signs, so we can attain, in writing, the swiftness "of the winged speech. But you, oh, youth, must make the signs "very carefully, and pay attention to an accurate arrangement of "them, as through a little mistake a long speech will be disfigured, "while by the care of the writer the speech may be correctly re- "peated."

Hieronymus relates that, on account of the feebleness of his eyesight, and principally in consideration of the condition of his health, he could not himself write, but that he dictated his thoughts to a tachygrapher, who, when he (Hieronymus) at any time reflected, in order to think of something better, impatiently frowned and reminded him by gestures that he was unoccupied. In this author's work many allusions are made to the employment of shorthand writers.

Evodius, Bishop of Uzalis, in Africa, who flourished about the year 420 A. D., refers in one of his letters to a young tachygrapher, who rendered him excellent service in his work.

C. Sollius Appollinaris Sidonius likewise mentions stenographers.

So does Gregory, the Great, who frequently availed himself of the aid of shorthand writers. He expressly states this in several passages of his writings. Anscharius, Archbishop of Hamburg in the 9th century after Christ, is said to have written down many things in tachygraphical signs to the praise of Almighty God and for the chastisement of the godless.

In addition, we must mention Epaphroditus, "lector" and shorthand writer to the Bishop Hellanicus, of Rhodes; Athanasius, the notary to Alexander; and Proclus, the notary to Bishop Atticus. Finally, Montfaucon refers to Buanes, notary to Archbishop Areta, of Cæsarea, and to a certain Varus.

Having thus shown how manifold was the employment of tachygraphy in the early Christian churches, we can still refer to other records which contain allusions to this art. If, in the second volume, second section of the "Dictionary of the Greek Language, "edited by Franz Passow," under the word "ταχυγραφέω, shorthand writing" is meant, quoting Tzetzes, this citation might be very questionable evidence for the history of our art. The passage in itself, as it appears, is so corrupt that a sensible translation seems scarcely possible, and we will, therefore, leave it undecided whether a stenographic writer could really be meant by the word ταχυγραφῶν. It is our opinion that it refers rather to quick, careless writing, than to stenography.

In consequence of the existing conditions and institutions of the Roman world, which were entirely different from the mediæval, as well as from modern times, the multiplication of books could be carried on in those times to the most stupendous proportions without costing much more than at the present time. This great multiplication was only possible through slaves, and what the printing press now accomplishes mechanically was performed then by hundreds or thousands of human hands. Even in Cicero's time, Pomponius Atticus made a business of this multiplication. He had among his slaves numerous laborers in every branch of the manufacture of books; he had some who glued and polished the papyrus; others who made envelopes artistically and elegantly; skillful copyists and stenographers, and, finally, experienced and learned correctors. It would lead us too far from our subject to here consider more fully the development and business of the book trade in the Roman empire—but we may consistently ask the question: "What had stenography to do with these branches of industry?" The answer is simply: "That this art influenced writing generally." There were numerous abbreviations from stenography incorporated into the common script; abbreviations which were universally intelligible. They were used most extensively in the greater part of the manuscripts of the ancient classics. The stenography of the ancients was similar to the common script, and probably the stenographic slaves were used at the same time for stenographing and for copying. As the readers were instructed in the right explanation, so the book-copyists were instructed and drilled in the proper employment of the stenographic signs in order to complete the copies in the shortest possible time; the use of more full word-forms was only required in books of elegant style. In this way the common editions could be very quickly prepared, as the reader, naturally, was very familiar with the meaning of the abbreviated signs. Of course the great number of mistakes in the manuscripts, of which Cicero complained, must be ascribed in part, at least, to the use of *siglae* and the Tironean Notes, which were often misunderstood or inaccurately copied, giving rise to misunderstandings and causing later critics to have much trouble with the disfigured texts.

If the ancient stenographers earned much praise, they were also severely punished. For instance, it was decreed that calygraphers and stenographers who copied the writings of the teachers of heretical doctrines should have their hands hewn off, and Aelius Lampridius relates that the Emperor Severus had the sinews of a notary's fingers cut on account of a falsification. It appears even that in certain cases the employment of the Tironean shorthand writing, which gradually crept into the manuscripts, was forbidden. Justinian commanded that the texts of the codes should not be written in signs or enigmatical abbreviations.

Gabelsberger says "that it is not decided whether this fre-
"quently repeated, but not always heeded, edict was also directed
"against the employment of the Tironean Notes or any system
"of a shorthand writing in judicial and other proceedings;" but,
if we consider that the transcriber, in order to do his day's work
quicker, used signs and commonly known Tironean Notes in the
text, and, as Kopp says, that traces of such signs really exist among
the abbreviations used in judicial proceedings, the above mentioned
imperial decree must have referred to tachygraphical signs as well,
in the broader sense.

The order of the Emperor Basilius, quoted by Gibbs, from the
Cedrenos, does not, apparently, apply in this connection. In that
command the employment of the abbreviations for numbers was forbidden, and it was ordered that they should be so written that every
countryman could read them.

We will now undertake to say a few words concerning the social
standing and the reputation of the ancient tachygraphers. The
record from these earlier times is, for the most part, not at all edify-
ing. *Notarii*, as well as *librarii*, were, as Kopp says, the most uncultivated people. Seneca, as we have already mentioned, calls them
the lowest slaves, and if the expression of Cicero, which we
have likewise alluded to, refers to tachygraphers, severe cen-
sure must fall upon their performances. Kopp truly observes
that if they were educated it is very certain that they did
not write without making mistakes. The necessity for quickly
noting down upon the wax tablets what they heard left them no time
to observe the orthography. They stenographed according to the
hearing, rather than according to the sense. It should be added
that through the carelessness of those dictating, the words which
were pronounced otherwise than written, were not noted in full,
but abbreviated. Julius Firmicus Maternus, of Sicily, (336 A. D.)
and others reproach tachygraphers as being malevolent dishonest
vagabonds in every respect—scurrilous words which can scarcely be
justified.

We have yet to mention a noteworthy thing, namely : how high
a value was placed upon a shorthand writer. Justinian valued one at
about sixty dollars. Apart from what has been mentioned, it
appears from a letter of Bishop Synesius, which speaks of a
ἀρχὼν τῆς συμμορίας τῶν ταχυγράφων by the name of Marcus,
that stenographers at a later time must have enjoyed a certain prominent station. As an example—if we may be permitted in this case
to translate ὑπογραφεὺς as a shorthand writer—Trotz, the commentator of the works of Hugo on the origin of writing, mentions a certain Procopius, figuring in a speech by Themistius, who, under the
Emperors Valentinanus and Valens, obtained great dignity and
honor.

As to the so-called *notarii ecclesiastici*, we have already spoken of them when mentioning the services which the tachygraphers had rendered by reporting the sayings of the martyrs.

Finally, as regards the credibility of the tachygraphical reports, it was considered that they did not deserve full confidence until they had been entered in the records. This closely resembles our custom of to-day, when the verbatim report of the stenographer has no official character, although it no doubt offers a better, because a more objective and complete picture of the speech than the official record.

To give a clear and comprehensive statement of the social standing of the tachygraphers of the olden times, we must, if possible, penetrate the darkness which still hovers over the art of writing among the Romans.

In regard to the materials used by stenographers we will briefly state the following : In ancient times, in place of our memorandum books and pencils, small wooden tables, provided with raised margins, were used. These were laid over with a thin coating of wax— *tabulae ceratae, cerae, codicilli, pugillares*—on which the writing was scratched with a metallic, or bone, pencil—*stilus, graphium,*—pointed on one end for writing, and the other end left blunt for erasing, (*stilum vertere*). These were used by scholars for writing down their thoughts and annotations, as well as by business men, for keeping book accounts, in housekeeping, and for correspondence. In fact, this appears to have been the most popular writing material. The custom of writing on such wax tablets continued, probably in consequence of its convenience, and especially on account of the easiness of the writing, almost to our time. What wonder, therefore, that the shorthand writers made use, almost exclusively, of the wax tablets and styluses, several of which were generally bound together—hence the name, *diptychi, triptychi,* &c.

The employment of the kind of writing material just mentioned was, unquestionably, a great loss of information to posterity. As soon as a speech was stenographed and transcribed the wax was rubbed smooth in order that another might be taken down on the same surface, while the transcribed speech was elaborated and published. To the best of our knowledge, no real stenographic writing has been transmitted to us ; we know only the elaborate products of the oratory of those days. What a loss to the examiner of the historical domain of tachygraphy! What a loss to the study of the oratory of the ancients !

Here we can only allude briefly to the character of the Tironean Notes. For a more accurate knowledge of the ancient tachygraphy we must refer our readers to the very copious and often cited work by Kopp, as well as to the excellent works of Professor

Wilhelm Schmitz, of Cologne, which have been published in the
" Panstenographikon," and in the Reinisches Museum for Philology,
under the title " Tironiana," in the *Symbola philologorum Bonnensium.*

The so-called Tironean Notes originated, as Kopp has plainly
proven, from the majuskeln—Latin capital letters—with which are
mixed several Greek letters. These, naturally, through the haste of
the tachygraphers, were often abbreviated and mutilated even to un-
discernibleness, and their form changed after they were combined
with this or that sign, or even written in a different order.

Only such parts of the capitals were employed as appeared necessary for the designation of a word. A capital letter, which was mostly,
but not always, abbreviated and simplified, either stood in the place
of a whole word, or a sign was added which represented the end-
ing ; or there were two or more parts of the capitals placed together,
or with the addition of small terminal signs united in one stroke,
which represented either the endings, the tenses of the words, or
helped to distinguish cognate words from one another. Those
larger capitals, representing the root or the radical of a word are
called *signa principalia ;* while the smaller signs representing the
terminations or tenses placed below, above, to the right or to the left
of the *signum principale*, are the *auxiliaria*. These smaller signs consisted either of parts of capitals, or of lines and points. This
ancient tachygraphy, representing through the *signa principalia*
and *auxiliaria*, whole words or even whole sentences (which may
be called *verbalis*) we must distinguish from the *syllabaris*, by which
syllables only are designated.

It is very evident that, in the ancient practice, a certain oscillation
in the mode of abbreviation was common among the fraternity, and
that the latter, in the haste of writing, did not pay too strict attention
to orthography, but represented frequently occurring words by one
sign and involuntarily left unrepresented immaterial parts, syllables,
words, common phrases, which could easily be replaced by the context. That the demotic writing of the Egyptians exerted an influence on the ancient shorthand writing, as has recently been maintained, we decline to accept. There may have been abbreviations
used in the hieroglyphics—as everywhere—but this, in principle is
very different from stenography. It is not demonstrable that any
similarity exists, especially in such simple forms as those used for
o, e and z. For, even in German writing, we can trace something
resembling the forms of Arabic letters.

The demotic writing is an abbreviation of the writing with short-
ened or rude pictures, of the second power ; it may include, as all
writings do, word-signs, (our ciphers are indeed, of the same nature),
but we cannot convince ourselves that between it and the Roman
shorthand writing there is any connection.

As regards the tachygraphy of the Greeks, Kopp denies, and successfully proves his denial, that the Roman shorthand writing was probably borrowed from the Greeks. This view is in opposition to that of Lipsius, Carpentier and Amati, whose opinions Gabelsberger supports, in so far as he believed, "that the idea of the art "of shorthand writing of the Greeks had passed over to the "Romans, and that Tiro having obtained some knowledge "of tachygraphy, directed himself, especially during his next "sojourn with Cicero in Athens and Eleusis which was "chiefly devoted to science, to improving his knowledge." But closer investigation into the character of both systems, their similarity and differences, clearly shows that the former opinion is absolutely unfounded. "The Greek notes, as well as the Ro-"man, consist of majuskeln. If one considers this, and remembers "at the same time that the Latin and Greek letters (because of one "origin) are even now similar, and were formerly still more so, we "can easily find a reason for that similarity, without believing "that one writing grew out of the other. And again, in spite of all "similarity in the arrangement of the letters, and in the transposi-"tion of the signs, &c., there exists such an extraordinary difference "between the two ways of writing that it cannot be supposed the one "originated from the other." That single signs had passed from the Greek to the Roman tachygraphy can readily be admitted, but there is nothing remarkable about that, because Roman shorthand writers must frequently have been compelled to write Greek. Kopp believes that Greek tachygraphy did not originate until the third or fourth century. He believes this on account of the similarity which exists between the tachygraphic signs and the letters in manuscripts of the second and third centuries.

In modern times, Dr. Lehman, a member of the Royal Stenographic Institute, has made a specialty of Greek stenography. The result of his investigation is, that neither the time of the first appearance of stenography in Greece, nor the time of its decline, can be determined exactly. We have, however, given sufficient evidence in the numerous foregoing instances and data quoted, that Greek shorthand writing found manifold practical applications. As to the question, whether the writing in the manuscript 3,032 of the Paris Library is really a sample of note-writing which the Greek shorthand writers used, Lehman denies. It should also be noticed that the Tironean Notes differ from the Greek, principally because the word-forms of the latter were written by syllables, and not, as the former, with one stroke. Aspirates and accents were added.

Manuscripts in Tironean Notes have not come down to us from ancient times. Whatever is preserved of the kind is from the pens of the notaries, who used the tachygraphic forms, but were not able to comprehend the substance of the same. Hence, the frequent intermixing of common writing with the stenographic, and the inaccurate word-forms of later times.

The Tironean Notes were no longer *scriptura literalis*, they had grown to be a *scriptura realis*.

If we go into details concerning what has been preserved in Tironean Notes, we must first consider the collection of commentaries on Roman tachygraphy, of which we find a treatise in the appendix to *Inscriptiones Antiquae totius orbis Romani*, published in 1603, in Heidelberg. by Gruter, (*ex-officina commeliniana*); the appendix being part of a sort of compendium under the title : "*Notae Tullii Tyronis ac Annaei Senecae sive characteres, quibus utebantur Romani veteres in scriptura compendiaria ubi Litera verbum facit.*" The notes were published a second time in the same year ("*iterum*," says Gruter in the dedication), and again as a supplement to the work in the Seneca edition, by Andreas Schott, under the title : "*Notae Romanorum veterum quibus litera verbum facit Tullii Tyronis Ciceronis liberti, et Annaei Senecae; Erutae nunc primum e bibliotaphiis editaeque a Jano Grutero. Ex officina Commeliniana CIƆIƆCIII.* A commentator says of Gruter's work : *Si quem dura manet sententia judicis olim Damnatuum aerumnis suppliciisque caput; Hunc neque fabrili lassant ergastula massa, Nec rigidas vexant fossa metalla manus : στενογραφήν texat; nam cetera quid moror? omnes Poenarum facies hic labor unus habet.*"*

" If we consider this collection more critically," says Dr. Krause,
" we find that the first commentary begins by explaining the steno-
" graphic designation of prefixes—prepositions—then it proceeds to
" indicate their combination with the most usual verbs, which con-
" stitutes almost a third part of the whole work. In the passage
" where Isidor says that Tiro had written a commentary on stenog-
" raphy, he adds, *sed tantum praepositionum*—but only for the
" prepositions, and, therefore, appears to intimate that in the com-
" pendium, which he (Isidor) knew, the first commentary, is the one
" that Tullius Tiro edited. The title of this work agrees completely
" with this declaration. The same work, as we now have it, com-
" prises a great collection of commentaries from different times ;
" the last of which was written in the Christian era, and every-
" where we find traces of alterations and additions made at dif-

[*The appendix being part of a sort of compendium under the title : "Notes of Tullius Tiro and Annaeus Seneca, or characters, which the ancient Romans were in the habit of using in abbreviated writing, where a letter represented a word." * * * * And again, as a supplement to the work in the edition of Seneca, by Andreas Schott, under the title : "Notes of the ancient Romans, by Tullius Tiro, a freedman of Cicero, and Annaeus Seneca, now brought forth for the first time from the libraries, and edited by Janus Gruter, in which a sign stands for a word. From the Commelian collection (more literally ' workshop) of— * * * *
A commentator says of Gruter's work : "If a hard judicial sentence fell upon any one, in older times, he was punished by torture (or hard labor) and death. Let not the inmates of the house of correction harrass such a person hereafter with the tools of the artisan, and let not his hands be pained with harsh metallic instruments ; let him work at (out?) stenography. Why should I stop to say more? This labor contains within itself all forms of punishment.]

6

"ferent times. Probably at the time, when Christianity became
"the predominant religion, everything obsolete and paganish was
"expunged from the commentaries and replaced by the newly-
"formed Christian expressions, so that the number of written charac-
"ters remained about the same."

. No refutation is necessary for the assumption of Abbot Joannis, of
Tritenheim, that Cicero wrote a treatise on stenography.

Undoubtedly the question is only one concerning a manuscript of
those commentaries, the principal part of which is Tiro's work.
Abbot Joannes relates that he, in the year 1496, from his love of books,
searched through several libraries, and found, in a cloister of his order,
a neglected and dusty copy of it, and exchanged it for a printed copy
of the work of St. Anselm, which he had bought " for the sixth part
of a florin." From this manuscript Abbot Joannes abstracted thirty
Tironean characters and incorporated them in his Polygraphy.
When Abbot Joannes makes the statement that Thascius Caecilius
Cyprianus, Bishop of Carthage (256 A. D.), multiplied the commentaries on the Tironean Notes by signs for newly-formed words for the
use of Christians, and, therefore, made the work more useful and ac-
ceptable to the believers, he asserts what he fails to prove, and the
editors and commentators of the writings of that martyr know nothing of such a circumstance. In opposition to this statement, W.
Schmitz (*Tironiana 540*) is of opinion that Trithemius could not
justly ascribe this action to St. Cyprian without better evidence; and,
as great Christian influence was exercised in the editing of the notes,
and the interest in stenography was not less in the old church than
in our days, so it may be possible that the active Bishop of Carthage
had labored on the Notes, and had obtained from the Trithemius
manuscript a positive statement to some such effect, but that that manuscript has been lost, according to all accounts of later times, or at
least, until now it has not been discovered. Tritenheim designates the
" *Dictionarium*" obtained by him as a complete collection of Tironean
Notes. The number of the same was so large that they were sufficient to take down anything that one would wish to write. Kopp
surmises that St. Eligius published a similar collection of Notes:

The basis of the edition by Gruter was two manuscripts, while
Kopp, more fortunate than his predecessor, found the lost key to the
Roman tachygraphy contained in seven manuscripts, which he used
when composing his "Tachygraphy of the Ancients." Of these manuscripts he considers the one preserved at Cassel the most ancient,
dating back in the 8th century. The examination of the Wolfen-
büttler manuscript, the great value of which the librarians Ebert
and Schönemann mention, was not granted to the zealous investiga-
tor. Dr. Krause (to whom, through the proposition of the directors
of the Royal Stenographic Institute at Dresden, the necessary means
were supplied by the Minister of the Interior to enable him to go to

Wolfenbüttel to examine and copy this manuscript at the library there) characterizes the "*Lexicon notarum Tironianarum*" as excellent in every respect. The writing was neat and correct, and the text more complete and more correct than the one given by Gruter.

If, by the way, it has been said that Sueton wrote a work on the Notes, which has been supposed by many to be a dissertation on or compendium of the Roman tachygraphy, this supposition is certainly an error. The writing of Sueton in question περὶ τῶν ἐν τοῖς βιβλίοις σημείων treats of the critical signs of the grammarians.

The Psalms appear to have been written in Tironean Notes by way of preference, and these often served, as it appears, for practice in writing. It is, therefore, no wonder that such collections of Psalms written in Roman shorthand writing have come down to us. Kopp knew of three ; he examined two of them which were in Paris, and which originated in the 7th and 9th centuries. He could not get permission to read the manuscript at Wolfenbüttel. Yet, Dr. Krause has fully copied this manuscript, and afterwards carefully compared it with the original. It is to be found now in the library of the Royal Stenographic Institute at Dresden. "It does not merely contain the " Psalms, but also seventeen pages of different songs of praise from " the Old Testament, the *oratio dominica*, the *symbolum apostolorum*, " and the *fides catholica Athanasii* (*Quicumque vult*), all written in the " Latin language and the Tironean Notes. The entire manuscript is " beautifully written, so that from this book, more than from the " above mentioned (Wolfenbüttel) code, we recognize the real form " of the stenographic signs of the Romans, which appears often dis- " figured in Gruter, and is likewise faulty in Kopp. It is the intention " to print, by the zincographic process, both these manuscripts in the " Wolfenbüttal library : the so-called *Lexicon Tironianum*, as well as " the one mentioned here, so they may be of service to the sten- " ographic public, as well as paleographers, philologists and theolo- " gians, because the text, written in Latin and in the Notes, by no " means harmonizes everywhere with the Vulgate, and, besides, it " would be of interest to compare these texts of the Athanasian creed " with the one more generally known."

"The vicissitudes of this codex are remarkable. Augustus, Duke " of Brunswick, after whom a most complete collection of codices, " Augustei,' is called, prepared an autograph catalogue of the Wolf- " enbüttel library, which is still in existence and is especially inter- " esting as regards the Tironean Notes. In the Wolfenbüttel copy " of Gruter's edition of the notes there is a passage in which Abbot " Joannes of Tritenheim relates that he saw in the Strassburg library a " psalter written in the Tironean Notes, on the margin of which is " the following observation in the Duke's handwriting : ' *Invenitur* " ' (*hoc psalterium*) *jam in libraria affinis Ducis Pomeraniae Philippi*,

" '*cui dono dedi*' to which was subsequently added : ' *Recepi post*
" '*obitum ejus.*' The psalter which is preserved at the present time
" in Wolfenbüttel is the same that Trithemius saw and described in
"Strassburg in 1498." A similar book of Psalms is to be found in
the library of St. Germain des Prez.

Moreover the following, written in Tironean Notes, are to be mentioned : Diplomas and a capitulary of Louis the Pious, a letter of
Chrysostomus to Demetrius *de compunctione cordis.* Dr. Bethmann, a
co-laborer on Pertz's *Monumenta Germaniae*, in the library of Val-
enciennes, found a noteworthy employment of the Tironean Notes.
On the inside of the binding of a manuscript of the 10th century,
entitled *Paradisus Smaragdi, de conversione S. S. Putrum*, there was
a fragment of a homily on the prophecy of Jonas in a vulgar
dialect, mixed with Latin, in which all the Latin and a few words of
the vulgar idiom were written in Tironean Notes. (Pertz Archiv
VIII. 442.)

Kopp further quotes *Hyginus de siderbius* (in the Library at Paris)
and Isidor (in the Vatican Library); a manuscript of Curtius with
marginal and concluding observations in the Tironean writing in
Bern ; a *breviarium Alarici* in Munich with Tironean marginals.

Again, Gabelsberger mentions a copy of the Salic law, which was
formerly in the library at Beauvais, but now probably to be found in
Paris.

The Tironean Notes are also to be found in the following manuscripts :

1. A book (*Codex Ovitensis* 58) which was formerly in Oviedo, but
now in Madrid, which begins with a genealogical table of the Gothic
kings. These Madrid notes are given in full and described in W.
Schmitz's " Study of the Latin Stenography " in Panstenographikon,
Vol. 1.

2. Codex of Lactantius *de opificio dei*, in quarto, which was first at
Bobbio, but which, we regret to say, is not now to be found.

3. Two codices of the Leyden university (*Vossianus Lat. O.* 94 *et*
Q. 98.)

4. The manuscript of Isidor from the 9th century, No. 9311-9319,
which formerly belonged to the Jesuits at Antwerp, but which is
now in the great library at Brussels.

5. The manuscripts No. 190, 7493, 8777, 8778, 8779, 8780 in the
library of Paris.

6. Manuscript No. 85 in the library at Geneva.

7. The Lexicon *Tironianum* of the Göttenger ecclesiastical library,
which Theo. Sickel has described in the report of the proceedings of
the philosophical and historical sessions of the Vienna Academy.
Vol. 38 part 1, 1861.

8. Two Bern codices 358 and 668, which W. Schmitz likewise expressly described and reproduced in Vol. 1, of the Panstenographikon.

9. One fragment at the Wolfenbüttel Library, mentioned by W. Schmidt in his " *Tironiana*," one leaf and a half from a manuscript in Tironean Notes from the ninth century.

10. A list of *Dies Aegyptiaci* in Tironean Notes, to be found on the back of folio No. 99 in the Wolfenbüttel manuscript of Tironean Notes.

The manuscript of Tironean Notes formerly kept in the Strassburg Library was destroyed by fire at the burning of the library, but the text of the same was preserved in a copy made by W. Schmitz September 4–8, 1869, in the library above mentioned, containing the printed collection of Gruter. This codice is described in detail in the Rheinisches Museum for Philology, N. F. xxvi P. 146, etc. An inspection of the supposed codice existing in Oxford has proved it to be a worthless transcript made in the 17th century from the Gruter collection. A manuscript, superscribed *Diomedes grammaticus et liber de notis*, which was hastily examined by the author at the library at Paris, contained on the last page a collection of the Tironean Notes, which end with Placiat. At the close of the manuscript we read : *Explicit prologus de vulgaribus notis, quem ego J. Grosselinus hic transcripsi ex alio libro manuscripto hujus bibliothecae*, 1598.*

It is possible, however, that there are many undiscovered manuscripts written wholly or in part in Tironean Notes which may some day meet the keen search of a paleographer.

On the Latin codices in the National Library at Paris under the catalogue numbers 190, 7493, 8777, 8778, 8779 and 8780 there are 6, which, with the exception of the last designated parchment manuscripts of the *Commentarii notarum*, are partly complete and partly fragmentary, in quarto. Schmitz, after a personal inspection and comparison with the notes printed by Gruter, published in the Rheinisches Museum for Filologie, Vol. 31, p. 287, etc., a more accurate report than Kopp was able to give in his work, Vol. 1, p. 301. Schmitz establishes the succession of the various codices relating to this subject in the following manner : Codex Cassellanus from the second half of the eighth century, and the Paris manuscript 190, constitute the first and most valuable group. Next we have the commentary in the first Gruter manuscript, the Paris manuscript 8779 and the Leyden codices O. 94 and Q. 93 as the second group. The Göttweiger manuscript, the Paris manuscripts 8777 and 8780 and the Strassburg manuscript as the third ; and finally the Paris manuscript 8778 as the fourth group ; while the Geneva and the

Paris manuscript 7493 cannot be placed in any of these groups. In a further article on the Tironean Notes, contained in the same volume of the Rheinischen Museum für Filologie, p. 631 etc., Schmitz says, respecting the words of Muratori in dissertation *de notariis* (*Antiq. Ital medii aevi I*): " *Mihi in Ambrosiana Mediolanensi Bibliotheca non unus Codex hisce Notis scriptus sese obtulit, quas cum contulissem cum evulgatis a Grutero easdem ipsas esse deprehendi, atque inde recte deducebam verba per ejusmodi Notas scripta,*"** these expectations are based on the belief that there must exist codices written in Tironean Notes in the Ambrosian library, and gives it as his opinion that Muratori does not say that the Milan codices written in Tironean Notes contain the Gruter text of the *Commentarii Notarum*, but intimates from authentic sources, that these note commentaries do not exist in the Milan library in manuscript form. The only codex in Tironean Notes is the Ambrosianus M. 12, sup. seac. ix, a palimpsest—the ancient writing in uncial letters contains a missal—whose superscription reads: " *Incipit liber bede de temporibus et variis temporum spatiis.*" The text is for the greater part written in Tironean Notes, and in such a way that on many pages only a few notes are interspersed, whilst in others the stenographic mode of writing preponderates.

There appears to be but little of the Greek stenography preserved to us. Kopp cites two manuscripts, one preserved in the Vatican Library which contains among other works written in the usual writing, the works of Dionysius Areopagita and a portion of the book Henoch written in Greek shorthand ; and a second, included in the writings of Hermogenes of Tarsos, and others (161 A. D.), which is found in the Paris Library.

The manuscript of the rhetoric of Hermogenes, much used in classical authorities, is the principal source of the knowledge of Greek tachygraphy. The German philologist Bast, in Paris, secured for Kopp an inspection of this manuscript and under his direction the writing was soon deciphered. Montfaucon in his Paleographia Graeca had caused two tables from this manuscript to be engraved, and endeavored to explain the writing ; but as the signs had not been made exact enough and Montfaucon had not hit the true sense, Bast decided to engrave in copper these " rhetorical signs," as they called these writings, for the reason that they were in a book on rhetoric, and charged Kopp with the execution of this plan. Kopp spent all possible time on this work, but, unfortunately, Bast died before it was completed.

If we look for the one who, in the course of time, after the stenography of the ancients had ceased to be employed and had become a

---

** " In the Ambrosian Mediolan library, not a single book came into my hands written " In those notes which, having been compared by me with those published by Gruter, " I did not find to be the very same; and then I straightway concluded that the words " were written in characters of this kind."

mystic-like writing, was most active in searching for the key to it,— we find him without doubt to be the oft-mentioned Abbot Tritenheim, who first published a few Tironean signs. Baptist Porta followed him, and in his treatise on secret writing gave three such stenographical signs engraved on wood. An unknown author also, later on, gave some specimens. Lipsius wrote his celebrated letter to Leonhard Lessius about this note writing. The letter of Cardinal Bembo to Pope Julius, in which he asked him to do everything to revive the study of the Tironean Notes, should not be passed without mention. After Gruter had published in his above mentioned work a large collection, Mabillon, Montfaucon, Carpentier, Toustain and Tassin, rendered service by the publication of and efforts at explanation of the Tironean Notes, but Ulrich Kopp, a well-known paleographer and Hessian Cabinet counselor, succeeded, after long researches made with German thoroughness, in lifting the veil from this hitherto deeply buried treasure of antiquity, and presented to the astonished world the key to the Roman and Greek tachygraphy. His work, often mentioned by us, stands to this hour as an invaluable monument of German learning and German acumen, though later researches have shown a few occasional errors in it. It should be stated, however, that the wooden types of the numerous Tironean signs contained in the work which he caused to be printed, (which were executed at his own expense) are still preserved, as we learn, in the possession of the antiquarian Bär at Frankfort-on-the-Main.

After Kopp, Tardiff occupied himself with a close study of Tironean Notes.

At the present time Wm. Schmitz, director of the college at Cologne, has, above all, rendered service by the explanation of the character of the Tironean Notes.

Tironean Notes were also used for signatures, amongst others, in a deed of record issued by Bishop Agius in the year 854 to the canon of St. Aignan respecting the erection of the chapel of Notre Dame du Chemin, which is to be found in the Antiquités Historiques de l'Eglise royale de Saint-Aignan d'Orléans par M. Hubert, Chanoine de S. A. 1664. Jules Tardiff took the pains to explain the Tironean Notes occurring in that document.

The knowledge of Roman tachygraphy (which in the Middle Ages was only known by the name of Tironean Notes) as well as the knowledge of the Greek, dates from the 9th century after Christ. It was, however, still in use during the rule of the Carlovingians. It was used for paraphs in diplomas, for signatures to decrees and for the signing of important manuscripts, such as collections of psalms and formulas, as well as for sketches of judicial writings. Perhaps it served also at that period to fix the winged word, which may be inferred from a passage in a letter of the Abbot Hilduin. In the 10th century it was entirely lost.

48

STENOGRAPHY FROM THE TENTH TO THE END OF THE SIXTEENTH CENTURY.

Dubiae crepuscula lucis.

In former historical essays these centuries have been passed over very hastily. Anders makes several allusions to the subject, but always in a doubtful manner. Neither are we able to present irrefutable proofs of the existence of stenography during this period. Still, we consider it a duty, in accordance with those allusions, to present a few points which may be an aid to further investigations. Alluring as is the temptation, we refrain from adducing any hypotheses in favor of the existence of our art in all that time because of the following facts:

Abu Muhammad Ben Ishak, relates in his complete History of Literature,—which is one of the oldest in possession of the Arabians,—in the year 987:

To Abu Bekr Muhammad Ben Zakarjâ ur Razi—the Rasis or Rhases yet celebrated in the medical world, who died in the year 923 of our era—a man came from China and resided about a year with him, and acquired the Arabian language and writing within five months. A month before his return to his native country, he requested his teacher to have dictated to him sixteen certain books of Galenos. To the objection made that the time was far too short to do it, the Chinaman replied: By no means, dictate as fast as you can, I will keep up with the words. The scholars of Rhases dictated as rapidly as they possibly could, but he wrote still faster and surpassed them all. The former, in astonishment, asked him how that was possible. He answered, we have a writing which we employ when we want to write much in a short time. I used this kind of writing. When it is necessary, we transcribe this writing into the common or ordinary writing. But he added, significantly, even one who is intelligent and quick of comprehension will require at least twenty years of continual study to master that writing.

From this interesting report, although unsupported by stronger evidence, we can reasonably infer that the Celestials had a stenography.

Besides we find a similar instance in Haji Khalfa's encyclopediacal Lexicon of bibliography much resembling that given in the above cited *Fihru*. We do not venture to assert the opinion whether or not both narratives may be identical, and that Haji Khalfa has only inaccurately given what he found in his authority.

On the other hand, that stenography was not known to the Arabians, is to a certain degree astonishing, but, according to Haji Khalfa, is positively assured.

It would not be out of the way to mention, in this connection, the "broken writing" of the modern Persians. They possess a special writing approaching stenography which is frequently employed by them in ordinary life, and which is not easily read by foreigners otherwise well acquainted with the Persian language.

Khalfa, professor in the *Collège Arménien-Moorat* in Paris, gives in his " *Guide de la conversation* " (Paris 1854) for stenographer the Turkish word " *Hátti moukhtassar yazan* "—one who writes with abbreviations—but the matter itself is unknown in Turkey.

Anders mentions a certain Abbot Eckard in St. Gall who was a skilful shorthand writer. My predecessor probably did not have anything else in view than the notice given in Kopp's work (P. 485) that Ekkehard (died 973) the dean of the abbey at St. Gall, through his " *Notulae*," amazed the Emeror Otto Second. But Kopp does not venture to decide whether or not any Tironean shorthand writing is to be understood by this *notulae*.

In the life of St. Bernard (1091–1153) it is related that God, whilst the choir sang, opened his eyes and that he saw an angel standing next to the monks, who, as a kind of shorthand writer, truly noted down what the former sang.

We are especially indebted to Valentin Rose of Berlin, for the statement, that on the soil upon which shorthand writing of modern times originated, namely, in England, centuries before, in the second half of the twelfth century, an attempt at a complete system of stenography had been made which, like modern stenography, is in marked contrast to the notes of the ancients—a stenography which was termed *nova notaria*, as differing from the long perished and forgotten *ars notaria*. The time from the tenth to the sixteenth century is no longer a blank page in the history of stenography. The author, John of Tilbury, considers himself the first inventor. He pretends to serve especially the needs of the *scholares;* he has at the same time the highest idea of the importance and success of his invention, through which in the twinkling of an eye, the scholars will equal the teacher ; through which a sure foundation will be acquired for a more comprehensive mastery of existing knowlege and of its effective extension,—*ut unicuique vel de quacunque re interrogetur semper aliquid respondendum habeat prae manibus.** Outside of England this " *ars notaria aristotilis* " appears to have been scarcely known. It is embodied in several manuscripts, one of which is preserved at Florence ; the best and most complete is at Oxford, and a third at London. The author guards against the confounding of this art with the magical arts. He pretends to be indebted for it to suggestions of St. Thomas. He describes the art as follows : *Ejus vis et efficacia est velocitas scribendi docere ut ea celeritate, qua ex ore verba proferuntur, pari quoque velocitate voluntis manus notarias excipiantur, ita ut non praevenit os*

[*" That he might have something ready to respond, whosoever might question " him concerning any subject."]

7

loquentis manum notarii, sed praecurrens manus notarii semper anticipet os loquentis, si talem cum impetu verba non fundantur. * He further says that he had previously explained his new writing in three volumes; two comprising the theory and analysis of his new system through conversations between *notarius* and *amicus*, and one on practice, which contains a dictionary of the notes. Of these books we know nothing. What lies before us is a kind of abridgement in the form of a letter. In the introduction there is a criticism on the *antiqua notaria.* Those examples which John of Tilbury produces as characterizing the Tironean Notes indicate, however, according to Schmitz, that the English monk either possessed a mangled text, or had an incomplete knowledge of the Tironean Notes. He assigns, as technical terminations, the words *nota*, and *titula*, for the principal sign and for the auxiliary signs. In his system, an alteration of the letter " I," through different beginnings of a cross stroke, designates the twenty, or rather the nineteen fundamental letters of the *notarial* alphabet, and from the same I, through points (and by round and tailed strokes), and points added to it, in various positions, are formed the multiplicity of the note figures and all the *titulae.* From the uncertain and even deficient context of the letter and the absence of the aforesaid three complete books, we can form no correct idea of the whole matter nor of what it accomplished. It is a question whether this invention in the main, was really more than an amusement of the cloister cell, or whether it was perfected in the mind of the author. Finally, as regards the author himself, Mr. Rose has only the following to say : John of Tilbury was a monk and a clergyman, a learned man and an author, but was sickly and suffered especially with his eyes. He did not write the letter preserved to us before 1174, and probably not very long afterwards.

Above all, the question which it is important to answer is, whether shorthand writing was known in the old universities and was made use of in them. In this connection we find the following facts : " Not an unimportant part of the present existing commentarial lit- "erature," says Savigny, " consists of college note books. Even " among the several commentators of the earlier times, individual " students were known as collectors and editors. Indeed Nicolaus Furiosus, the pupil of Joannes Bassianus,"—who flourished in Bologna in the latter part of the 12th century,—" undertook that work." He gained great credit, as is further related, by a verbatim annotation and the dissemination of the lectures of his teacher.

["* The power and efficacy of this is rapidity in writing, to show that words are repeated by the hands of a rapid reporter with the same rapidity with which they are uttered ; so that the speech of the speaker shall not outrun the movement of the hand of the reporter, but the hand of the notary, running ahead, may anticipate the speech of the speaker, if the words be not uttered with vehemence."

" Now, although I am incensed and irritated to no purpose that my thoughts, uttered at breakfasts and dinners, are given to the public, I am even compelled, by the entreaties of other friends, to adorn whatever I have to say with a preface, although I have nothing—unless, as I do not care to deny—my words, even, have been thought out."]

" This same service was rendered Azo (died 1230) by Alexander de
" Sancto Aegidio, who mentions it in the preface to the printed lec-
" tures of Azo concerning the Codex. Likewise the best and the
" most important writings we have of Odofredus (died 1256)—his
" exegetical writings—and which secured for him a lasting fame, are
" lectures written down by the hearers and subsequently circulated
" in real books. The correctness of this opinion appears from the
" character of that work, wherein the hearers are constantly ad-
" dressed with: *or signori*. The positive appellation *lecturae*, further
" confirm, this, while the commentary of Accursius is constantly named
" *apparatus*. This explains the extraordinary difference of the hand-
" writings, which could not easily have occurred in real books."

The confidential and vivacious tone, but also the negligence which
characterized many of these lectures, the rendition of all phrases,
memorial verses and jocular remarks, and the referring of the audi-
tors to their own study of the passages which had been omitted in the
lecture : all this testifies still further to the literal rendering of the
lecturae. On the other hand it supports the assumption that the lecture must have been delivered entirely extemporaneously by the
teacher.

" The exegetical writings of Guidos de Suzaria, one of the theo-
" rists (died between 1283 and 1292 at Bologna), which, according to
" Accursius, relate to the code, exist in manuscripts in Paris, are
" likewise not commentaries, but are reported lectures. The con-
" clusion of one of them reads : *Nec dico plura hic, quia tarda hora*
" *est.* Perhaps two of his pupils, Jacobus de Arena and Guido de
" Baisio, wrote down these lectures."

The greater part of what we have of Bartolus (died 1357) are likewise *lecturae*, many of which were preserved merely because they
were taken down by hearers.

" In the twelfth and fifteenth centuries almost the entire legal lit-
" erature was condensed by this method of procedure."

Also, in other universities, writing down lectures was a daily exer-
cise, for which Savigny presents a remarkable proof, especially regarding the practice at the university of Paris. That this custom
was also observed in the medical school at Salerno, is highly probable, although proof of it is lacking at the present time.

Quétif and Echardet, the publishers of the *scriptores ordinis
praedicatorum* state that among those manuscripts preserved in Sar-
bonne, there are lectures delivered by Albert the Great (died 1280)
which were taken down by the most nimble fingered hearers.

A hint that in the thirteenth century shorthand writing was in use
is derived by the Italian authors from the well known passage in
Dante's Divine Comedy (Paradise, Canto 19, Line 133), in which the

poet alludes to the avaricious king Frederick of Sicily, son of Peter of Arragon :

> Et a dare ad intender quanto è peco,
> La sua scrittura fien lettere mozze.
> Che noteranno molto in parvo loco.

The mode of preaching of the 13th and subsequent centuries also offers to the investigators in our field many interesting facts.

Thus, it is related of the Franciscan monk Bertold, one of the most popular of all men who lived and worked before and after his time in Germany, that most of his sermons delivered in the open air before an almost incredibly large crowd of people, and which sermons are acknowledged as the most excellent of the German homilies of the thirteenth century, uniting rare vivacity and freshness of substance as well as form of delivery, were written down by hearers.

Indeed, Jacob Grimm says : "I must say, further, that I consider "it was written down with the utmost reliability, and that the pecu-"liarities of the orators in phraseology, expressions, and even in the "dialects were accurately comprehended. If the orator himself had "written out his sermons he would, perhaps, have polished and con-"tracted the periods, and thereby deprived them of their natural-"ness, which, to the reader as well as the hearer, however, was the "most delightful and attractive part."

"There is no doubt of the possibility," continues our author, "of "a faithful and complete reporting of a recently delivered ser-"mon from memory by intelligent hearers. Such is the case even in "our day; how much more in those times, when the powers of mem-"ory, on the whole, were more acute and concentrated, and the prac-"tice of writing down was held in a proportionately higher estima-"tion. In Tauler's (died 1361) sermons (old edition printed at Leip-"zig) there is mentioned a sermon which was fully noted down by a "hearer."

"Since Tauler, Strasbourg, nay, entire Germany, has seen no "popular preacher of such brilliant qualities that his sermons were "universally received as oracles, none who so earnestly and candidly "exercised his calling, as Johann Geiler, of Kaisersberg, (died 1510). "His sermons, originally composed in Latin,"—which he, as Beatus Rhenanus says, had hastily written down at home—"were, as he him-"self never published anything, for the most part published by the "Franciscan monk, Johannes Pauli, (1506–1510, guardian of the "*Minorite* Convent at Strasbourg) ' who wrote down as much as he "'remembered of every sermon.' Jacob Wimpheling, Joh. Adel-"phus (city physician at Schaffhausen) and Henry Wessmer have "also translated several of his series of sermons into German."

Wickgram, Geiler's nephew and successor in the office of preacher, as well as Jacob Other and Beatus Rhenanus, edited a part of Geiler's orations in the original writing. The just mentioned relative of the great pulpit orator speaks in a very deprecatory manner of Pauli's publications, whether from envy, because the latter anticipated him, or from policy, in order to render less conspicuous some passages reflecting upon the clergy that would thus aid in preserving the good standing of his uncle in the church.

In *Thomae a Kempis vita Florenti, cap. 23*, we find the statement that the numerous scholars whom the fame of Florentius (died .1400) drew to Deventer, noted down the words of the master, in order to send them to distant friends.

Joannes Gerson (really Charlier, of Gerson, or Jerson, a village in the diocese of Rheims, died 1429), Geiler's teacher, diligently preached in his native language. His numerous sermons were written down by devout hearers and transcribed into the French language, not verbatim, but according to the sense, and were subsequently translated into Latin. But the peculiar charm of freshness and originality, according to Wimpheling's preface (A. D. 1401), unfortunately became lost in the transcriptions.

We read further that the sermons of St. Bernhardin, of Siena (15 in number), delivered in the year 1427 in the public market of the city, were written down by a citizen of Siena named Antonio de' Bartolomei, a cloth cutter by trade, upon wax tablets (*in tavolette de cera*) and invariably engrossed on the same day.

The style of the sermons is clear and ingenious, simple and temperate, not obscured through deficiencies which characterized the Italian language subsequent to the time of the 15th century. The words are in a large part peculiar to the dialect of Siena, which was familiar and very valuable to the saint from his youth, until the Crusca, in expunging them, deprived the sermons of their richest bloom.

Abbot Luigi de Angelis supposes that it must have been an easy thing for the shorthand writers to follow the rapid discourse verbatim, even in a standing position, and without support, and surrounded by the pious multitude. "The tablets," says he, "render "sufficient resistance, they were easy to turn, occupied little space "and once covered with wax received every impression. In the past "centuries they made use of those tablets covered with wax in order "to accomplish what modern tachygraphers accomplish with paper "and pencil. The former process would present no difficulty even "in our days, as it appears that Benedetto di Bartolommeo in the "15th century got along very well with it." "The tachygraphers," adds de Angelis, "expressly employed signs and abbreviations in or- "der to write quicker, and this art of shorthand writing has extended "to our days, although it did not come into universal, nor even into "frequent use."

A great part of the sermons of the "new prophet," Girolamo Savonarola, (died 1498) were reported by the worshipers, especially by a Florentine "notary" by the name of Lorenzo di Jacopo Violi. In all the older editions of his sermons this fact has been mentioned in the words : "*Raccolte dalla viva voce.*" "The natural force and "energy of the language of Savonarola often affected the hearers so "powerfully that not only the multitude broke out in loud crying, "but even men like Pico della Mirandola were not unfrequently "awe-struck by the power of his oratory and his convincing employ-"ment of biblical passages." Violi was once so overcome with weeping while reporting, that he was, on that account, unable to write until the close of the sermon.

What wonder that such sermons were written down and circulated in copies ! To be sure, in doing so it frequently happened that many discourses were abbreviated incompletely on account of haste, and were taken down with many inaccuracies : others, from the want of proper understanding, or even from malicious design, were disfigured by additions and omissions, and were spread through the community, and even made public in print. For that reason Savonarola felt the necessity of protesting before the people in a special pamphlet (*compend. rece'att.*) against that sort of publication of his discourses.

Likewise, the table talks of the great reformer, Luther, (died 1546) were taken down "from his mouth." In the preface to the "Collo-quies, or Table Talks of Dr. Martin Luther," (first put in print by Joannes Aurifabrus Vimarienses A. D. 1566, and printed at Jhena by Tobias Steinmann,) we read : "And belong to this *praecl. dep.* "*script. rec. patr. Lutheri,* also these *fragm. colloq.* or *serm. memorial.*. "which many highly learned and pious men, who lived with and "near Dr. Luther, and his disciples and friends, among them Vitus "Theodorus, Antoninus Lauterbach, Wellerus, Rorarius, Mathesius "and others, diligently and truly noted down ' from the mouth' of "the holy man of God,"

Luther acknowledges the correctness of these reports as follows : "*Nunc etsi frustra indignor et irascor esse in publicum raptas*" (*sc. cogitationes sub prandiis et coenis effusas*) "*cogor etiam, aliorum ami-*"*corum precibus, praefatione ornare, cum tamen nihil habeam, quid* "*dicere possum, nisi quod negare non audeo, mea esse et cogitata et* "*verba.*"

Myconius relates of Luther's contemporary and co-laborer in the work of reformation, Dr. Cruciger, (or Creutziger): "It has never "been heard that any man on earth could have written so fast as this "Dr. Cruciger, and when he wrote down and extracted from the ser-"mons or lectures of Luther, he forgot no word, so that all the world "was astonished at it."

Dr. Löhn, in his below cited work, repeats this statement, and still further explains "that Cruciger had used, for greater accuracy, ab-"breviated signs intelligible only to himself, which he subsequently, "as stenographers now do, supplied to the copy through ordinary

"syllables and words, and was, therefore, prepared in a short time
"afterwards to present the oral lecture to Luther almost without de-
"ficiencies. Many a word of genius and strength spoken by the
"inspired man, which was called out on the spur of the moment,
"must have been lost to posterity, had not Cruciger's skill and untir-
"ing zeal preserved and accurately communicated them to us.
"However, as Cruciger was not quite satisfied with the accuracy of
"his transcripts, and feared that in the hurry many a sentence was
"not heard, or was incorrectly understood, he instructed his friend,
"George Röhrer, in this art. Both now reported Luther's lectures
"and sermons at the same time, then compared with each other what
"they had put on paper, and mutually sought to complete the re-
"port."

During the religious dispute between Eck and Melanchthon, held in
the year 1540 at Worms, "Cruciger, through his above mentioned
"skill, wrote down almost every word of Melanchthon and Eck with
"incredible swiftness, and frequently prompted the former, who was
"still suffering from the effects of his illness, if he had forgotten to
"bring forward anything in his answer to the latter's objections.
"Chancellor Granvella (who presided over the Reichstag) could not
"wonder enough concerning this rapid gift of conception and re-
"markable dexterity in bringing the spoken words immediately to
"paper with the greatest accuracy, and at last expressed his aston-
"ishment in the words : 'The Lutherans have a writer who is far
"'more learned than all the Roman Catholics.'"

Whether the "new and peculiar letters" which Jewel, Bishop of
Salisbury (1559), made use of in composing his numerous and
comprehensive common-place books were only of the nature of secret
signs, and not shorthand writing, we shall not decide. It has been
supposed, however, that they were the latter, and this is not entirely
improbable.

When Gabelsberger says, " information and traces of the employ-
" ment of tachygraphy for the recording of the proceedings of state
" assemblies have descended from the most ancient times, especially
" notable in the Storthings of Norway, in the legislative proceedings
" of Sweden, in the Cortes in Spain, and in the Parliament in Eng-
" land," he has neglected to give us the sources from which this information is derived. We ourselves have not been able to find any
evidence thereof. Anders also maintains that there was no reliable
information on that point.

Many examples of political oratory from the golden age of Polish
literature (1506 to 1622) are preserved to us. As Sigismund, the elder,
towards the end of his reign (1506 to 1546), had issued a " Wizje "
(general summons) and when all the *voivodeships* in the neighborhood of
Lemberg (Lwów) had convened, the numerous assembly—which

opened at the break of day and deliberated in the open air—very soon forgot the original object of their coming together (the decision of the question whether or not the Wallachians could be brought to subjection by force), and proceeded "to debate according to the "rules of ancient oratory, and observed all the forms of modern dis- "cussions. The speeches delivered during these deliberations are "accurately preserved to us by the historians. Christendom here saw "for the first time an example of parliamentary oratory." Among those who carefully collected the voting and addresses "as some thing important and remarkable," it appears that Orzechowski, pre- bendary in Przemysl (died 1570), took the lead. It is a pity that our authority, the celebrated Mickiewicz, says nothing, or has nothing to say, of the manner in which those monuments of oratory of his countrymen were written down and collected. We cannot think of stenography being employed there.

When we sum up everything that has been said in the foregoing, we may repeat that, aside from the *ars notaria* of John of Tilbury, from the decline of the Tironean Notes to the 16th century, stenog- raphy, in its true sense, was not known and practiced; on the other hand, it cannot be denied that occasionally the threshold of this art was almost crossed.

www.ingramcontent.com/pod-product-compliance
Lightning Source LLC
Chambersburg PA
CBHW022030080426
42733CB00007B/794